THiNK

WORKBOOK 3

Herbert Puchta, Jeff Stranks & Peter Lewis-Jones

B1+

T0349636

CAMBRIDGE
UNIVERSITY PRESS

Acknowledgements

The authors and publishers acknowledge the following sources of copyright material and are grateful for the permissions granted. While every effort has been made, it has not always been possible to identify the sources of all the material used, or to trace all copyright holders. If any omissions are brought to our notice, we will be happy to include the appropriate acknowledgements on reprinting.

Cambridge University Press for the text on p. 61 from 'The Mind Map Level 3 Lower-intermediate' by David Morrison. Copyright © 2009 by Cambridge University Press. Reproduced with permission of Cambridge University Press;

Experience project for the text on p. 76 from 'I Got Caught Shoplifting'. Copyright by Experience project. Reproduced with permission of Experience project;

Random History for the text on p. 94 from '99 Valuable Facts About', 2013. Copyright © 2013 by Random History. Reproduced with permission of Random History;

Cambridge University Press for the text on p. 115 from 'Bullring Kid and Country Cowboy Level 4 Intermediate' by Louise Clover, 2010. Copyright © 2010 by Cambridge University Press. Reproduced with permission of Cambridge University Press.

Corpus

Development of this publication has made use of the Cambridge English Corpus (CEC). The CEC is a computer database of contemporary spoken and written English, which currently stands at over one billion words. It includes British English, American English and other varieties of English. It also includes the Cambridge Learner Corpus, developed in collaboration with Cambridge English Language Assessment. Cambridge University Press has built up the CEC to provide evidence about language use that helps to produce better language teaching materials.

English Profile

This product is informed by the English Vocabulary Profile, built as part of English Profile, a collaborative programme designed to enhance the learning, teaching and assessment of English worldwide. Its main funding partners are Cambridge University Press and Cambridge English Language Assessment and its aim is to create a 'profile' for English linked to the Common European Framework of Reference for Languages (CEF). English Profile outcomes, such as the English Vocabulary Profile, will provide detailed information about the language that learners can be expected to demonstrate at each CEF level, offering a clear benchmark for learners' proficiency. For more information, please visit www.englishprofile.org

Cambridge Dictionaries

Cambridge dictionaries are the world's most widely used dictionaries for learners of English. The dictionaries are available in print and online at dictionary.cambridge.org. Copyright © Cambridge University Press, reproduced with permission.

The publishers are grateful to the following for permission to reproduce copyright photographs and material:

T = Top, B = Below, L = Left, R = Right, C = Centre

p. 6: ©Goodluz/Shutterstock; p. 14: ©karelnoppe/Shutterstock; p. 15: ©Monkey Business Images/Shutterstock; p. 22: ©The Art Archive/Alamy; p. 24: ©VisitBritain/Britain On View/Getty Images; p. 27: Charles Dickens at the Blacking Factory, an illustration from 'The Leisure Hour', 1904 (engraving), Barnard, Frederick (1846-96) (after)/Private Collection/Bridgeman Images; p. 29 (TL): ©Becky Stares/Shutterstock; p. 29 (TR): ©Arcady/Shutterstock; p. 29 (CL): ©Vitezslav Valka/Shutterstock; p. 29 (CR): ©konstantinks/Shutterstock; p. 29 (BL, BR): ©Arcady/Shutterstock; p. 32: ©Fuse/Getty Images; p. 40: ©ITV/REX; p. 48: ©KIM NGUYEN/Shutterstock; p. 50: ©Lebrecht Music and Arts Photo Library/Alamy; p. 51: 'The Boy Who Biked the World' 'On the Road to Africa' (part 1) (Nov 2011). Published by Eye Books. Used with permission; p. 58: ©Bobby Bank/WireImage/Getty Images; p. 59 (TL): ©sauletas/Shutterstock; p. 59 (TC): ©Neirfy/Shutterstock; p. 59 (TR): ©Ryan DeBerardinis/Shutterstock; p. 59 (BL): ©Vladimir Caplinskij/Shutterstock; p. 59 (BC): ©SUSUMU NISHINAGA/SCIENCE PHOTO LIBRARY; p. 59 (BR): ©Lourens Smak/Alamy; p. 68: ©Rawpixel/Shutterstock; p. 69 (T): ©Jeremy Horner/Alamy; p. 69 (CL): ©HLPhoto/Shutterstock; p. 69 (CR): ©REX; p. 69 (B): ©ROMEO GACAD/AFP/Getty Images; p. 76: ©David Young-Wolff/The Image Bank/Getty Images; p. 78: ©Clarissa Leahy/Cultura/Getty Images; p. 83: ©Blend Images/Shutterstock; p. 86: ©Jarno Gonzalez Zarraonandia/Shutterstock; p. 87: ©Mary Evans Picture Library/Alamy; p. 89: ©Fulcanelli/Shutterstock; p. 90: ©Air Images/Shutterstock; p. 94: ©PjrStudio/Alamy; p. 98 (TL): ©Bragin Alexey/Shutterstock; p. 98 (TR): ©Julian Rovagnati/Shutterstock; p. 98 (BL): ©Robyn Mackenzie/Shutterstock; p. 98 (BR): ©Ivonne Wierink/Shutterstock; p. 99: ©Taina Sohlman/Shutterstock; p. 104: ©Neil Bradfield/Shutterstock; p. 105: ©KPA/Zuma/REX; p. 106: ©Paul Bradbury/Caiaimage/Getty Images; p. 109: ©Lisa Peardon/The Image Bank/Getty Images; p. 112 (L): ©Photo File/MLB Photos via Getty Images; p. 112 (R): ©Jon Kopaloff/FilmMagic/Getty Images; p. 113: ©Juanmonino/iStock/Getty Images Plus.

Cover photographs by: (TR): ©Stephen Moore/Digital Vision Vectors/Getty Images; (L): ©Andrea Haase/iStock/Getty Images Plus/Getty Images; (BR): ©Pete Starman/Stone/Getty Images.

The publishers are grateful to the following illustrators:

Bryan Beach (Advocate Art) 34, 69
David Semple 7, 28, 39, 42, 57, 85
Fred van Deelen (The Organisation) 20, 67
Julian Mosedale 11, 36, 55, 60, 109, 117

The publishers are grateful to the following contributors:

Blooberry: text design and layouts; Claire Parson: cover design; Hilary Fletcher: picture research; Leon Chambers: audio recordings; Karen Elliott: Pronunciation sections; Matt Norton: Get it right! exercises

CONTENTS

WELCOME

A MUSIC MAKERS
be allowed to / let

1 **Rewrite the sentences using the word in brackets.**

House rules: what my parents let or don't let me do.

0   My parents don't let me play loud music in my bedroom. (allowed)

   I'm not allowed to play loud music in my bedroom.

1   My parents let me stay up late at the weekend. (allowed)

   _____

2   I'm allowed to practise my electric guitar in the garage. (let)

   _____

3   I'm not allowed go out on school nights. (let)

   _____

4   My parents let me have parties at home. (allowed)

   _____

5   I'm not allowed to go to concerts on my own. (let)

   _____

Music

1 **Unscramble the words and write them in the correct list. Add two more items to each list.**

srumd | laslacsic | jzaz | oilniv
tagriu | opp | inapo | par

Musical instruments	Types of music
_____	_____
_____	_____
_____	_____
_____	_____
_____	_____

2 **Complete the sentences so they are true for you.**

1   I really like listening to _____

2   I never listen to _____

3   I play _____

4   I'd love to play _____

Verbs of perception

1 **Complete with the correct form of the verbs in brackets.**

1   Why _____ you _____ (smell) the milk?

2   What's for dinner? It _____ (smell) great.

3   What _____ you _____ (look) at?

4   You _____ (not look) great. What's the matter?

5   It _____ (taste) awful. What is it?

6   Why _____ you _____ (taste) the soup again?

7   **A**   Why _____ you _____ my coat (feel)?

    B   I'm sorry. It's just so soft.

8   I like the way this jumper _____ (feel) .

9   I love your new hairstyle. It _____ (look) fantastic!

10   Your hands _____ (feel) very cold. Are you OK?

11   She's _____ (not taste) the food for the wedding today; she'll do it tomorrow.

12   I don't like that new building. It really _____ (not look) good.

Big screen, small screen

1 **Do the word puzzle and find the name of the biggest film of 1997.**

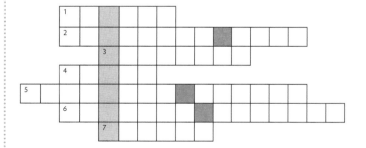

1   A film that is full of explosions and car chases.

2   A cartoon style film, usually for children.

3   An exciting film full of suspense.

4   A film with a powerful story.

5   A film that makes you laugh and maybe cry.

6   A film about other worlds.

7   A film that makes you laugh.

Present perfect tenses

1 Circle the correct form of the verb.

1 I haven't *watched / been watching* TV for more than a week.

2 I've *seen / been seeing* this film before.

3 The cinema has *shown / been showing* the same film for weeks now.

4 If you've *lost / been losing* your ticket, you can't come in.

5 They've *waited / been waiting* in the cinema queue for three hours.

6 You've *read / been reading* the TV guide for an hour. Can I have a look now?

TV programmes

1 Match the parts to make types of TV programme.

0	chat		com
1	game		programme
2	drama		show
3	sit		news
4	sports		show
5	the		series

SUMMING UP

1 Complete the conversation with the words in the list. There are three you won't use.

're watching | let | 've been watching | the news
jazz | allowed to | watch | to watch | watched
've watched | guitar | drama series

DANNY   Ben, it's my turn [1]_____ TV.

BEN   Just give me twenty more minutes.

DANNY   But you [2]_____ TV for more than two hours now. You're not even [3]_____ watch so much TV. Does Mum know?

BEN   Yes, she does. Anyway I'm almost finished.

DANNY   Yes but I want to watch [4]_____ and it starts in five minutes.

BEN   You can [5]_____ it later. I really need to see the end of this.

DANNY   What is it that you [6]_____ anyway?

BEN   CrimeWave

DANNY   What, that American [7]_____?

BEN   Yes, that's the one. It's the last episode in the series. I can't miss it. I [8]_____ all the others. I want to know how it ends.

DANNY   I'll tell you how it ends. The policeman's the murderer. Now [9]_____ me watch my show.

B TIME TO ACT

The environment

1 🔊02 Complete the sentences with the words in the list. Then listen and check.

smog | flooding | global warming
pollution | fumes | litter

1 With the Earth's temperature rising each year, many scientists now believe _____ is the biggest threat to our planet.

2 _____ from factories and cars are creating huge _____ problems and many of the world's largest cities are permanently covered by thick _____ .

3 There has been serious _____ across the area and many people have had to leave their homes.

4 I get so angry when I see people dropping _____ in the streets. Why can't they use the bins?

Question tags

1 Match the sentences and the tags.

1 You don't care about the environment, ☐

2 You campaign for the environment, ☐

3 Global warming is getting serious, ☐

4 The world's not going to end tomorrow, ☐

5 You didn't go on the protest march, ☐

6 You threw your rubbish in the bin, ☐

7 The Earth can't take much more, ☐

8 Science can find a solution, ☐

a	isn't it?	e	didn't you?
b	did you?	f	do you?
c	can it?	g	is it?
d	can't it?	h	don't you?

2 Complete with the correct question tags.

1 You're from Argentina, _____ ?

2 This is pretty easy, _____ ?

3 You know him, _____ ?

4 They played really well, _____ ?

5 They don't speak English, _____ ?

6 She's working in London now, _____ ?

7 He can't sing, _____ ?

8 He won't be late, _____ ?

9 You've been to Canada, _____ ?

10 I shouldn't have said that, _____ ?

Party time

1 Match the sentence halves.

Am I ready for the party? Well, so far …

1 I haven't found anywhere ☐
2 I haven't got permission ☐
3 I haven't drawn up ☐
4 So clearly I haven't sent out ☐
5 I haven't hired ☐
6 Or even got the money to pay ☐
7 I haven't decorated ☐
8 And I haven't organised ☐

a the guest list.
b the food.
c a DJ.
d a deposit for one.
e the room.
f from Mum and Dad.
g to have a party.
h any invitations.

Am I ready? Nearly.

Indefinite pronouns

1 Complete the sentences with the words in the list.

everything | something | everyone | nowhere
somewhere | anyone | no one | nothing

The party was terrible.

1 I didn't know _____ .
2 _____ I tried to speak to just ignored me.
3 There was _____ to eat at all.
4 You had to pay for a drink and _____ on the menu was really expensive.
5 I wanted to leave my coat _____ but there was no cloakroom.
6 It was so crowded there was _____ to sit.
7 I wanted _____ to do so I went to the dance floor.
8 But _____ wanted to dance with me.

Arranging a party

1 Complete the conversation with the words in the list. There are two you won't use.

something | everywhere | sent out
decorating | everyone | get | anyone
everything | hiring | nowhere
organising | anything

POPPY   So, Jake, is ¹_____ ready for the party tomorrow?

JAKE   I think so. I've just finished ²_____ the room and ³_____ the food.

POPPY   So there will be ⁴_____ to eat?

JAKE   Yes, and to drink.

POPPY   So who's coming? ⁵_____ I know?

JAKE   There'll be loads of people you know. I ⁶_____ about 30 invitations.

POPPY   That's a lot of people. Did you have to ⁷_____ permission from your parents?

JAKE   Of course, I'm having the party at our house.

POPPY   Is there ⁸_____ I can do?

JAKE   Well, you could bring some music with you. I'm not ⁹_____ a DJ.

POPPY   OK, I'll bring some music that will get ¹⁰_____ dancing.

SUMMING UP

1 🔊03 Put the dialogue in order. Listen and check.

☐ BOB   Of course there is. I'm organising a protest march for Sunday. Do you want to join me?

☐ BOB   That's a shame. But you could donate a bit of money, couldn't you?

☐ BOB   And I don't think the government will do anything about it.

☐ BOB   And that is why I think we should do something about it.

[1] BOB   I think the pollution in our city is getting worse each year.

☐ SUE   I'm afraid I left my wallet at home. Sorry.

☐ SUE   So do I. It's a real problem, isn't it?

☐ SUE   Neither do I. They never do.

☐ SUE   But there's nothing we can do, is there?

☐ SUE   I'd love to but I can't. I'm busy.

C A BIT OF ADVICE
Health

1 Match the sentence halves.

1 Take this medicine and you'll feel
2 I always get
3 Dad's going to hospital to have
4 Can you phone the doctor and make
5 Why don't you see
6 You need to take more

a sick when I travel by car.
b an appointment for me?
c a doctor about your headaches?
d exercise to lose some weight.
e better in half an hour.
f an operation next week.

2 Complete the sentences with the correct form of the phrases in the list.

take some exercise | feel sick | have an operation | make an appointment | get better | see a doctor

1 I hope you _____ soon.

2 Hello, I'd like to _____ with Dr. Hill.

3 He's _____ .

4 I think you need to _____ .

3 That dog needs to _____ .

6 I _____ !

Giving advice

1 Complete the advice with the missing words.

> I get really tired when I have to run.

1 You _____ take more exercise.
2 You _____ better see a doctor.
3 You _____ to lose some weight.
4 You should _____ eat so much.
5 You had _____ be careful.
6 You ought _____ join a gym.

2 Write one piece of advice for each of these people.

1 'I can't do my homework.'

_____

2 'I'm bored.'

_____

3 'I haven't got any money.'

_____

4 'I'm new at school and I don't know anyone.'

_____

Comparisons

1 Use the words in brackets and any other necessary words to complete the sentences.

1   The Oscars are _____ (important) award ceremony in the film industry.

2   The host wasn't _____ (funny) the guy who did it last year.

3   The ceremony was a lot _____ (long).

4   The best actor's speech was _____ (bad) I can remember.

5   However, I think the actors were dressed _____ (beautiful) than usual.

6   Apparently one actress was wearing _____ (expensive) dress in the world.

2 Rewrite the sentences so that they mean the same thing.

1   It's hotter today than it was yesterday.

Yesterday wasn't _____

2   I've never seen a more boring film in my life.

That was _____

3   She's the kindest person I know.

I don't anyone as _____

4   I used to remember things more easily when I was younger.

I don't _____

5   Martin and Steve play tennis equally as well.

Steve plays tennis _____

6   It's the most expensive car in the world.

There isn't a car as _____

SUMMING UP

1 ◀))04 Put the dialogue in order. Listen and check.

	BRIAN	I'm going to. I've made an appointment.
	BRIAN	I'm not sure. Every day I wake up more tired than the day before.
	BRIAN	I know. I'm not sure I can wait that long.
1	BRIAN	I've been feeling really sick recently.
	BRIAN	The problem is it's for next Thursday. They didn't have one any earlier.
	VICKY	Oh dear. What's wrong?
	VICKY	You'd better call them and tell them it's an emergency.
	VICKY	What! That's a week from now.
	VICKY	Sick and tired. You should see a doctor.
	VICKY	Well hopefully he'll be able to help you get better.

D HELP!
Sequencing words

1 Rearrange the letters to make four sequencing words.

1   rafte _____

2   hent _____

3   yanllif _____

4   ta rifts _____

2 Use the words in Exercise 1 to complete the story.

1   _____ we thought we'd never get out. The door just wouldn't open.

2   _____ five minutes of kicking the door, we were exhausted.

3   _____ Dad found the key in his pocket.

4   _____ we got the door open.

Reported speech

1 Report the conversation.

0	JILL	I need help.
1	SUE	What's the matter?
2	JILL	I can't find my key.
3	SUE	Check inside your pocket.
4	JILL	I've already done that.
5	SUE	Have you checked the door?
6	JILL	Why do you want me to do that?
7	SUE	That's where you always leave them.

0   *Jill said that she needed help.*

1   Sue asked Jill _____

2   Jill said that _____

3   Sue told Jill _____

4   Jill said _____

5   Sue asked Jill _____

6   Jill asked Sue _____

7   Sue said _____

Asking for and offering help

1 Complete the words in the sentences.

1 Have you got a f_____ m_____?

2 C_____ I help you?

3 Can you l_____ me a h_____?

4 Could you h_____ me with something?

5 Do you n_____ any help?

2 Put the dialogue in order.

	MIMI	I said that I was going to tidy it after I'd done my homework.
	MIMI	What deal?
	MIMI	Could you help me with my homework?
	MIMI	That's the same deal we had before!
	MIMI	But you said you'd help me.
1	MIMI	Dad, have you got a few minutes?
	DAD	Tidy your room and then I'll lend you a hand with your homework.
	DAD	And you said you'd tidy your room – remember?
	DAD	That depends. What do you want?
	DAD	I'm sorry but I'm a bit busy.
	DAD	So I'll make you a deal.

IT vocabulary

1 Match the sentence halves.

1 Have you seen that Brian has posted ☐

2 Before you start you have to key ☐

3 I'm having a problem installing ☐

4 Send me the photo. You can attach ☐

5 I'm going to upload ☐

6 I'm sorry. I deleted your ☐

7 I'm not sure how to activate ☐

8 It's taking ages to download ☐

a all my holiday photos online.

b message. Can you send it again?

c the flight mode on this tablet.

d this program. Can you help?

e this file. It's really big.

f another message on the school website?

g it to an email.

h in your password.

Passive tenses

1 Rewrite the sentences using the passive.

1 Five people have posted new messages on my website.

Five new messages _____

2 Someone uploaded the video onto YouTube.

The video _____

3 Someone had already keyed in my password.

My password _____

4 Two million people have downloaded this video.

This video _____

5 No one activated the flight mode.

The flight mode _____

6 The program is attaching the file to the message.

The file _____

SUMMING UP

1 Complete the dialogue with words in the list.

files | said I | buy | has accessed | said he
passwords | has been | delete | installed
is being | then

LIAM My computer ¹_____ hacked.

KATE What do you mean, 'hacked'?

LIAM Someone ²_____ my computer from another computer.

KATE Really? How do you know?

LIAM A program has been ³_____ that has deleted loads of my ⁴_____.

KATE That's terrible.

LIAM And all my ⁵_____ have been stolen too.

KATE So what are you going to do?

LIAM My computer ⁶_____ looked at by an expert at the moment. He ⁷_____ could hopefully ⁸_____ the program.

KATE And if he can't?

LIAM He ⁹_____ 'd have to buy new computer.

KATE Well, if you do, remember to ¹⁰_____ some antivirus software.

LIAM Yes, and ¹¹_____ create some new passwords!

1 | LIFE PLANS

GRAMMAR

Present tenses (review) SB page 14

1 ★☆☆ **What tense? Write PS (present simple) PC (present continuous) PPS (present perfect simple) or PPC (present perfect continuous).**

0 I <u>haven't decided</u> what I want to do yet. **PPS**

1 I always <u>do</u> my homework when I get home from school. ___

2 Liam <u>hasn't been doing</u> well at school for a few months. ___

3 My sister<u>'s always talking</u> on her phone. ___

4 They<u>'ve been thinking</u> about buying a new house for more than a year now. ___

5 Jim<u>'s forgotten</u> to do his homework again. ___

6 Steve <u>doesn't want</u> to go to university next year. ___

7 It's the last week of term so we<u>'re not doing</u> very much at school. ___

2 ★★☆ **Complete the sentences with the words in the list.**

've been writing | don't write | 've played
's playing | hasn't been playing | plays
haven't written | 'm writing

1 No, he's not busy. He _____ cards on the computer.

2 I _____ my party invitations. Who should I invite?

3 Most people _____ letters, just emails.

4 I _____ all morning. My hand's tired.

5 My cousin usually _____ tennis twice a day. He loves it.

6 I _____ to thank my aunt for my present yet. I must do it tonight.

7 We _____ all of these games. Have you got any others?

8 She's not very good at the piano. She _____ for very long.

3 ★★☆ (Circle) **the correct words.**

We [1]*do / 're doing* some really important exams at school over the next few weeks so I [2]*spend / 'm spending* most of my free time studying for them at the moment. Normally the two things I [3]*like / 'm liking* most in life are TV and computer games but I [4]*don't watch / 'm not watching* any TV and I [5]*don't play / 'm not playing* computer games while the exams are on. I usually [6]*help / am helping* my dad in the shop at the weekends. He [7]*doesn't pay / isn't paying* me a lot but I [8]*like / 'm liking* getting the money. I [9]*don't work / 'm not working* there for a while. I [10]*need / 'm needing* the time for revision.

4 ★★☆ **Complete the conversations. Use the present perfect simple or continuous.**

1 A You look tired, Paula.
   B I am. I _____ very well lately. (not sleep)

2 A _____ your homework? (finish)
   B Nearly.

3 A Where's Bob?
   B I don't know. I _____ him for a few hours. (not see)

4 A You're dirty. What _____ ? (do)
   B Helping Mum in the garden.

5 ★★★ **Complete the conversation with the verb in brackets. Use present simple, present continuous, present perfect simple or present perfect continuous.**

JULES [0] *Have* you *seen* (see) Tara recently? I [1]_____ (not see) her for weeks.

DAN No, but she [2]_____ (text) me most days.

JULES So what [3]_____ (do) these days?

DAN Well, she [4]_____ (train) really hard for the past month.

JULES Training? For what?

DAN She [5]_____ (want) to be a professional footballer. Chelsea football club [6]_____ (invite) her to train with them. She starts with them on Monday.

Future tense (review) [SB page 15]

6 ★★☆ Look at Gillian's diary and write sentences about her plans for next week. Use the present continuous.

Monday	am: fly to Madrid pm: have meeting with Paulo
Tuesday	am: take train to Barcelona pm: watch football match at Camp Nou stadium
Wednesday	am: fly back to London

0 On Monday morning *she's flying to Madrid.*

1 On Monday afternoon _____

2 On Tuesday morning _____

3 On Tuesday afternoon _____

4 On Wednesday morning _____

7 ★★☆ Complete the sentences. Use a verb from the list and the correct form of *going to*. Then match them to the pictures.

~~see~~ | not visit | study | move | not ski | make

0 We *'re going to see* a play tonight. I've got the tickets.

1 The car's broken down. We _____ Grandma today.

2 I _____ a curry tonight. I've just bought all the ingredients.

3 Sue _____ Maths at Bristol University in September.

4 Paul has hurt his leg. He _____ today.

5 They are selling their house. They _____ to London.

8 ★★☆ Read the sentences. Write A for an arrangement, P for a prediction or I for an intention.

0 I've got a tennis lesson at 10 o'clock. `A`

1 I phoned the dentist and made an appointment to see him this afternoon. ☐

2 People living on the moon one day? Yes, definitely. ☐

3 We've decided where to stay in London – the Ritz hotel. ☐

4 I've decided what to do next year – travel around the world. ☐

5 My dad, let me go to the party? No way! ☐

9 ★★★ Rewrite the sentences in Exercise 8 using the correct future tense.

0 *I'm playing tennis at 10 o'clock.*

1 _____

2 _____

3 _____

4 _____

5 _____

10 ★★★ What do you think your life will be like when you are 30?

1 (be married) _____

2 (have children) _____

3 (live in a different country) _____

GET IT RIGHT! 👁

will vs. present continuous

Learners often use *will* + infinitive where the present continuous is needed.

✓ I**'m seeing** the dentist because my tooth is hurting.

✗ I**'ll see** the dentist because my tooth is hurting.

✓ I'm not sure we**'ll get** it done in time.

✗ I'm not sure we**'re getting** it done in time.

Complete the sentences with a verb from the list in the correct form.

~~come~~ | win | see | go | not go | have (x2)

0 It's good that you *are coming* to see me in Brazil!

1 We _____ a party next weekend – do you want to come?

2 I think Real Madrid _____ tonight.

3 My brother _____ to university next week. He's packing at the moment.

4 I _____ to his party later because I have to study for tomorrow's exam.

5 We think you _____ a great time on holiday.

6 Maybe I _____ you there.

VOCABULARY

Phrases with *up*

Making changes

make a resolution
give (something) up
do well
struggle with (something)
take (something) up
break a bad habit
form a good habit
change your ways

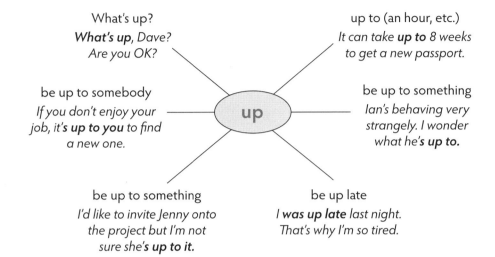

What's up?
What's up, Dave?
Are you OK?

up to (an hour, etc.)
*It can take **up to** 8 weeks
to get a new passport.*

be up to somebody
*If you don't enjoy your
job, it's **up to you** to find
a new one.*

be up to something
*Ian's behaving very
strangely. I wonder
what he's **up to.***

be up to something
*I'd like to invite Jenny onto
the project but I'm not
sure she's **up to it.***

be up late
*I **was up late** last night.
That's why I'm so tired.*

Life plans

leave school
get a degree
travel the world
start a career
get promoted
settle down
start a family
retire

Key words in context

arrangement	Who made all the **arrangements** for the party?
blame	Don't **blame** me for getting here late. I said we should take a taxi.
careers advisor	The **careers advisor** told me I should think about a job in politics.
criticise	Why do you always **criticise** everything I do? Do I never do anything right?
earn a living	He **earns a living** helping the elderly.
good intentions	He had a lot of **good intentions** at the start of the year but unfortunately he forgot most of them.
intention	I'm sorry I said that. It was never my **intention** to upset you.
leave (something) to the last minute	Maybe if you didn't always **leave your homework to the last minute**, you'd get better marks for it.
lifestyle	He has a very interesting **lifestyle**. He lives half the year in France and the rest in the USA.
prediction	I'm not going to make a **prediction** about this world cup because I think lots of teams could win it.
translator	My uncle is a **translator** at the United Nations. He speaks six languages.

Making changes SB page 14

1 ★☆☆ **Match the sentence halves.**

1 I've decided not to make ☐
2 I'm trying to give ☐
3 He's on a diet and doing ☐
4 I'm trying to get fitter but I'm struggling ☐
5 I need a new hobby so I've taken ☐
6 It's hard to break ☐
7 It's important for kids to form ☐
8 My dad needs to eat better but he's never going to change ☐

a really well. He's lost 5 kg already.
b with getting myself to the gym every day.
c good habits.
d his ways.
e up photography.
f up eating chocolate but it's so difficult.
g any resolutions this year.
h a habit sometimes.

2 ★★★ **Write down:**

1 a resolution you'd like to make for next year.

_____

2 something you'd like to give up.

_____

3 a school subject you do well in.

_____

4 a school subject you struggle with.

_____

5 a new hobby you'd like to take up.

_____

6 a bad habit you'd like to break.

_____

Life plans SB page 17

3 ★★☆ **Read the definitions and write the words and expressions.**

1 t_____ t_____ w_____ : go out and see other countries
2 g_____ p_____ : be given a better job (usually in the same company)
3 l_____ s_____ : finish compulsory education
4 r_____ : finish your professional life
5 g_____ a d_____ : graduate from university
6 s_____ d_____ : get married, buy a house, etc.
7 s_____ a f_____ : have children
8 s_____ a c_____ : begin your professional life

4 ★★☆ **Complete the sentences with the words and phrases from Exercise 3.**

1 My brother just loves being free. I can't see him ever wanting to _____ .
2 It's not easy to _____ a new _____ when you're 50.
3 The government wants to raise the age that you can _____ to 18.
4 I certainly want to _____ one day. I'd like at least three children.
5 I want to take a few years off work and _____ . I'd love to spend some time in Asia.
6 These days many people can't afford to _____ before they're 70.
7 I _____ from university but I've never really used it in my professional life.
8 If you work hard, you might _____ to junior manager next year.

WordWise SB page 19
Phrases with *up*

5 ★★☆ **Put the sentences in the correct order.**

☐ LINDA Why didn't you just go to bed?
☐ LINDA Really? What were you <u>up to</u>?
☐ LINDA Why? I don't understand.
1 LINDA <u>What's up</u>, Sam?
☐ SAM I was just playing video games with my dad. We were <u>up</u> until 1 am.
☐ SAM Well we were playing on the TV in my bedroom!
☐ SAM Nothing. I'm just feeling a bit tired. I was <u>up late</u>.
☐ SAM I wanted to but it wasn't <u>up to me</u>. I had to wait for my dad to finish.

6 ★★☆ **Match the underlined words in Exercise 5 with their meanings.**

1 doing _____
2 awake _____
3 didn't go to bed early _____
4 the matter _____
5 my decision / choice _____

Pronunciation

Linking words with *up*
Go to page 118. 🔊

READING

1 REMEMBER AND CHECK **Answer the questions.**
Then check your answers in the article on page 13 of the Student's Book.

1 What two resolutions has the writer recently made?

2 What has the writer done to try and lead a healthier life?

3 How is she finding it?

4 Why do scientists think we see our 'future self' as being different to our 'present self'?

5 How long does our brain need to get used to new habits?

2 Read the blog. How do SMART goals get their name?

SMART GOALS

It's that time of the year again that we all look forward to so much. Exams! (I'm using sarcasm here, of course.) Well this year I'm not afraid because this year I'm going to use SMART goals to make sure it all goes well. I read an article about SMART goals. They're what all successful people in life use, apparently.

So what are SMART goals exactly and how are they going to change my life (hopefully)?

Well SMART goals are Specific, Measurable, Attainable, Relevant and Timely. See how they get their names? No? Look at the first letter of each of the words. That's what you call an acronym.

Specific – because they are detailed. It's not good enough to simply say 'I'm going to revise for my exams.' That plan's too general. A specific goal is something like: 'I'm going to spend at least 20 hours revising for each subject and make a timetable to show exactly how I'm going to do this.' That is a Specific goal.

Measurable – because you should be able to measure your goals and ask yourself questions like: 'How much have I done?'; 'How much have I still got to do?'; 'How much time do I still need?'; 'Is this nightmare ever going to end?' Well, maybe the last one isn't such a great example, but you get the idea.

Attainable – because your goal should be something that you can actually do. If your goal is, for example, to raise £1 million for charity, write a novel, climb Mount Everest and revise for your exams then you might want to ask yourself if you really can do all this and then maybe drop one or two of them.

Relevant – because all your little goals should help you work towards your final one. So, for example, a plan to help your mum and dad with all the cooking, washing up and helping out with housework might make you the most popular child in your house but it's not really going to help you with the revision, is it?

Timely – Your goal must have a time frame. In other words, it must have a start and a finish. There's not much point if you're planning to finish revising a couple of weeks after your exams are over. That really doesn't make much sense. Likewise, you need to think about when would be a good time to start. And, as they say, there's no time like the present, I guess it might be a good idea to stop writing about SMART goals and start putting some into action. Goodbye.

3 Read the blog again. Mark the sentences T (true) or F (false).

1 The writer enjoys doing exams. ☐

2 The writer is going to use SMART goals to help her through her exams. ☐

3 SMART is an example of an acronym. ☐

4 SMART goals encourage people to do more than they can. ☐

5 You should plan a beginning and an end to your SMART goals. ☐

6 You don't need to think about when to start your SMART goals. ☐

4 Read the goal. Then follow the instructions.

'My goal this year is to be healthier.'

1 Make this goal more specific.

2 Write down what you can measure about this goal.

3 Write an example of an attainable plan and an unattainable plan for it.

4 Write an example of a relevant and an irrelevant plan for it.

5 Make a time frame for the plan.

5 Think of a goal you have and write a short paragraph about it. Is it a SMART goal?

DEVELOPING WRITING

An email about a problem

1 **Read the email. Who is …**

1 Dave? _____

2 Kev? _____

3 Conner? _____

4 Gina? _____

2 **Read the email again and answer the questions.**

1 What specific problems does Kev have with Conner?

_____

2 <u>Underline</u> the expressions that show you he's not happy with these things.

3 What plans has he made to resolve the situation?

_____

_____

4 (Circle) the language which introduces these plans.

3 **What does Kev do in each paragraph? Write a short description.**

A *He apologises for not writing and offers some excuses.*

B _____

_____

C _____

_____

D _____

Hi Dave,

A Sorry for not writing back sooner. I wanted to but I've been pretty busy with school work and football. Next week we're in the cup final – very exciting. Here's a photo of us at football training last week. We had just scored a goal! I hope you had a good time in Dubai – write and tell me what you did there.

B I've also been having a few problems at school recently with a new kid called Conner. The teacher asked me to look after him and I was happy to do that. The problem is that he's now decided I'm his best friend. He's always sending me text messages and wanting to hang out with me. I quite like him but if I'm honest I'm getting a bit tired of him following me everywhere. He also gets really jealous of my other friends and says some really mean things about them. Obviously, I'm not very happy about that!

C I know it's not easy moving somewhere new. So I've decided that I'm going to do something to help him (and, of course, help me too). Next week I'm having a welcome party for him so he can get to know some other people better and make more friends. I've also told him about the youth club and I think he's going to join it. The best part of that plan is that I can't go for the next few weeks because of football training so he'll have to hang out with other people. And finally I know Gina wants to meet him so I've given her his number.

D So that's my plan. If none of it works, I'm going to change my phone number! I'll write and let you know how it goes, but only if you write to me soon. Hope you're well.

From Kev

4 **Think of a person, real or imaginary, and write down three complaints about him / her. For each problem, think of a way of resolving it.**

problem	resolution
1 He's / She's always …	
2 The problem is …	
3 If I'm honest …	

5 **Write an email to a friend explaining your problems and what you're going to do about them. Write about 250 words.**

CHECKLIST ✔

☐ Introduction

☐ Explanation of problems

☐ Say what you're going to do about them

☐ Say goodbye

☐ Informal email language

LISTENING

1 🔊07 Listen to Lucy and Carla's conversation and complete the sentences.

1 Lucy is upset with _____.

2 Will promised to help her _____.

3 He arranged to meet her at _____ at her _____.

4 Lucy wants to study _____ at university.

5 The application needs to be in by _____.

6 Lucy asks Carla _____.

7 Carla says she's not good at _____.

8 Carla is _____ in the afternoon.

2 🔊07 Listen again. Complete these parts of the conversation.

1 CARLA What's up, Lucy?
  LUCY It's Will. _____ with him.

2 LUCY I can't believe he let me down.
  CARLA That's typical Will. _____ to do things and then forgetting.

3 CARLA Just text him and arrange another meeting.
  LUCY _____ the application needs to be in this afternoon.

4 LUCY Unless you could lend me a hand?
  CARLA I'd love to but _____ very good at that sort of thing.

DIALOGUE

1 Put the lines in order to make three short conversations. Write them in the correct spaces.

1 Making arrangements

A *Are you doing anything after school, Kim?*

B _____

A _____

B _____

2 Talking about future intentions

C *When do you finish school, Ping?*

D _____

C _____

D _____

3 Making personal predictions

E *Do you think you'll have children one day?*

F _____

E _____

F _____

1 I'm going to study medicine at Cambridge University.

2 Two or three.

3 Probably. I hope so.

4 I'd love to, thanks.

5 Ian and I are going swimming. Do you want to come?

6 Next year in July.

7 How many do you think you'll have?

8 And what are you going to do next?

9 No, I've got nothing planned.

PHRASES FOR FLUENCY SB page 19

1 Put the words in order to make phrases.

0 silly / be / don't   *Don't be silly.* _____

1 go / we / here _____

2 you're / star / a _____

3 hiding / have / been / where / you _____ _____ ?

4 start / where / I / shall _____ ?

5 mention / you / now / it _____

2 Complete the conversations with the expressions in Exercise 1.

0
A Shall we invite Jim to the game with us?
B *Don't be silly.* _____ He doesn't like football.

1
A You look busy. Have you got a lot to do?
B Busy? _____ I've got exams all week, I've got to organise Sue's birthday, buy her a present …

2
A Can I make you something to eat?
B Thanks. I'm starving. _____, Julia.

3
A I haven't seen you for weeks, Dave.

_____

B Nowhere. I've just been really busy.

4
A I know you've got to study for your exams but would you like to come for a quick bike ride?
B Well, I am busy but _____, it might be a good idea to get out for a while.

5
A Boys, get in here, you're 10 minutes late!
B _____ We're in trouble now.

Reading and Use of English part 1

1 For questions 1–2 read the text below and decide which answer (A, B, C or D) best fits each gap. There is an example at the beginning (0).

Teenage resolutions

According to a recent survey, more than 75% of 16-year-olds **(0)** _____ at least one resolution at the beginning of each New Year. The most popular ones are **(1)** _____ better at school and being nicer to family members. Other common resolutions include spending less time watching TV and giving **(2)** _____ playing computer games altogether.

0	**(A)** make	**B** do	**C** form	**D** find
1	**A** studying	**B** making	**C** revising	**D** doing
2	**A** in	**B** over	**C** out	**D** up

Exam guide: multiple-choice cloze

In a multiple-choice cloze, you read a short text in which eight words have been blanked out. For each of these you have to choose one of four options to correctly complete the space. This question is designed to test your knowledge of vocabulary including idiomatic language, phrasal verbs and prepositions.

- First of all read the text through without worrying too much about the missing words. It's always a good idea to get an understanding of the meaning of the text as a whole.

- Now focus on each gap in turn. Look carefully at the whole sentence that it is in, and especially at the words that come before and after it. Maybe you can guess what the word is without even looking at the options. If you can and your guess is one of the options then this means you've probably got the correct answer.

- If you can't guess the missing word then look at the four options you are given. Place each one in the space and read the sentence to yourself. Which ones sound wrong? Cross these answers out and concentrate on the others. Make your final choice by going for the one that sounds best to you.

- Finally if you really have no idea, then just choose one. Never leave an empty space on your answer sheet.

---

2 For questions 1–8 read the text below and decide which answer (A, B, C or D) best fits each gap. There is an example at the beginning (0).

Decisions

I'm just about to start my final year at school and I still haven't **(0)** _____ what I want to do when I finish. I come from a family where everyone has gone to university and I think it's probably what my parents expect me to do too. But, of course, it's not **(1)** _____ to them; it's my decision and the problem is I'm not at all sure what I would choose to study there. When my parents went to university it was free. The government paid for them to get a **(2)** _____ . Although both of them went **(3)** _____ to have successful careers, neither of them actually used the subject they studied. These days it's different. To go **(4)** _____ university is going to cost me at least £27,000 and that's only the course **(5)** _____ . I can't afford to study for a degree that I don't **(6)** _____ up using. I need to choose the right course and, as I said before, at this time in my life, I've no idea what that might be. If I'm honest, I'd like to take a few years **(7)** _____ to do some work and maybe travel the world. Perhaps with a little more life experience I'll be able to make a better decision before I **(8)** _____ down and start my career.

0	**(A)** decided	**B** thought	**C** settled	**D** fixed
1	**A** in	**B** for	**C** up	**D** out
2	**A** degree	**B** test	**C** form	**D** diploma
3	**A** forward	**B** on	**C** by	**D** further
4	**A** through	**B** by	**C** from	**D** in
5	**A** price	**B** fees	**C** fines	**D** bill
6	**A** start	**B** finish	**C** begin	**D** end
7	**A** over	**B** on	**C** out	**D** more
8	**A** live	**B** settle	**C** calm	**D** go

2 HARD TIMES

GRAMMAR
Narrative tenses (review) [SB page 22]

1 ★☆☆ (Circle) the correct form of the verb.

1 He *was / had been* tired because he *had run / had been running*.

2 My mum *was / was being* angry because I *was watching / had been watching* TV all afternoon.

3 My friends *played / had been playing* football for hours when I *arrived / was arriving*.

4 We *had been waiting / were waiting* for the concert to start for half an hour, when they *made / were making* the announcement.

5 My sister *was learning / had been learning* French for six years before she *went / was going* to France.

6 We *swam / had been swimming* for about an hour when it *started / had started* to rain.

2 ★★☆ Complete the sentences with the past simple or past continuous form of the verbs. Then match the sentences to the events.

0 Her car ___*was driving*___ (drive) through a tunnel in Paris when it ___*crashed*___ (crash).

1 It _____ (sail) across the Atlantic Ocean when it _____ (hit) an iceberg.

2 People _____ (dance) in the streets after they _____ (hear) he was finally free.

3 The world _____ (watch) on TV when Neil Armstrong _____ (step) on the Moon.

4 The crowds _____ (wave) at the president when they _____ (hear) the gunfire.

5 While people in the neighbouring town of Pripyat _____ (sleep), a nuclear reactor _____ (explode).

6 While Amelia Earhart _____ (work) one day, Captain Railey _____ (ask) her to fly to the UK from America.

Events that shook the world

☐ Chernobyl disaster (1986)
☐ Apollo 11 (1969)
☐ John F. Kennedy assassination (1963)
☑ *0* Death of Diana, Princess of Wales (1997)
☐ Freedom for Nelson Mandela (1990)
☐ Sinking of the *Titanic* (1912)
☐ First woman to fly across the Atlantic (1928)

3 ★★☆ Complete the sentences. Use the past perfect and the past simple once in each sentence.

Yesterday afternoon I had a guitar lesson.

0 When I ___*had finished*___ (finish) my guitar lesson, I ___*walked*___ (walk) home.

1 We _____ (have) dinner after I _____ (arrive) home.

2 I _____ (do) the washing up after we _____ (eat) dinner.

3 When I _____ (finish) the washing up, I _____ (call) my friend Tina.

4 I _____ (do) my homework after I _____ (speak) to Tina.

5 When I _____ (finish) my homework, I _____ (watch) a film.

4 ★★★ What did you do yesterday? Write similar sentences as in Exercise 3 using the past perfect and the past simple.

1 Yesterday afternoon I _____
_____

2 When _____

3 _____

4 _____

5 _____

18

would and *used to* SB page 25

5 ★☆☆ **Complete the sentences with verbs from the list.**

go (x2) | have | live | work (x2) | die | get up

In England in the nineteenth century …

1 Many children used to _____ in factories and mills.
2 They used to _____ very early in the morning.
3 They didn't use to _____ to school.
4 They used to _____ very long hours.
5 They didn't use to _____ nice food to eat.
6 They didn't use to _____ on holidays.
7 They didn't use to _____ very long.
8 They used to _____ young.

6 ★★☆ **Complete the sentences about yourself with *used to* or *didn't use to*.**

When I was five, …

1 I _____ go to a different school.
2 My mum _____ wake me up at 7 am.
3 I _____ eat cereal for breakfast.
4 I _____ walk to school.
5 I _____ have a lot of homework.
6 My dad _____ read me a bedtime story every night.

7 ★★★ **Tony is asking Anna about her primary school. Write the questions. Then match the questions to the answers.**

0 Which / school / go / to
   Which school did you use to go to?

1 wear / school uniform
   _____

2 have / a lot of homework
   _____

3 learn / English
   _____

4 learn / any other languages
   _____

5 What / favourite / subject
   _____

a It used to be Maths. ☐
b Yes, I used to learn French. ☐
c Yes, I used to be really good at it. ☐
d I used to go to Middleham Primary School. ☐
e No, I used to wear my regular clothes. ☐
f No, I didn't, our teacher didn't use to give us much. ☐

8 ★★☆ **In three of the sentences you can use *would* or *wouldn't*. Tick them and rewrite them using *would*.**

1 I used to be overweight. ☐
   _____
2 I used to play football every evening after school. ☐
   _____
3 I didn't use to like chocolate but now I do. ☐
   _____
4 I used to eat vegetables with each meal. ☐
   _____
5 I used to be very good at English. ☐
   _____
6 I used to go for a long bike ride every weekend. ☐

GET IT RIGHT! ◉
used to and *usually*

Learners sometimes confuse *used to* and *usually*. We use *used to* to refer to events which happened regularly in the past.

✓ *When I was at college, I **used to** work in a clothes shop.*

We use *usually* to refer to events which happen regularly in the present. We do not use *used to* for this.

✓ *I **usually** go to the cinema on Wednesdays because it's cheaper.*

✗ *I used to go to the cinema on Wednesdays because it's cheaper.*

Complete the sentences with *used to* or *usually* and the verb in brackets in the correct form: present tense or base form.

0 I *used to live* (live) in a really small village and I really liked it.
1 We _____ (sing) in shows together when we were younger.
2 These days I _____ (go) to bed early.
3 They _____ (watch) TV on Wednesday evenings because that's when their favourite programme is on.
4 Could you give us the 10% discount that we _____ (get) in the past?
5 He is more attractive than he _____ (be).
6 Do you _____ (wear) that funny hat?

VOCABULARY

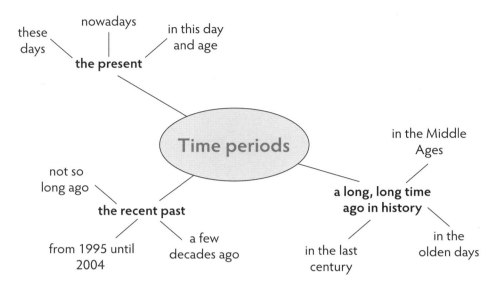

- these days
- nowadays
- in this day and age
- **the present**

Time periods

- in the Middle Ages
- **a long, long time ago in history**
- not so long ago
- **the recent past**
- from 1995 until 2004
- a few decades ago
- in the last century
- in the olden days

Descriptive verbs

dive

flee

rage

scream

demolish

smash

grab

Key words in context

accuse	They **accused** him of lying.
break out	The fire **broke out** just after midnight.
catastrophe	What's happened is a **catastrophe** for the whole country.
disaster	The earthquake was one of the worst **disasters** that ever happened in that area.
elderly	Our neighbour is a kind **elderly** woman.
fight a fire	It was difficult to **fight the fire**. It was so big.
flame	There was a big fire; people could see the **flames** for miles.
fuel	Wood, coal and petrol are different kinds of **fuel**.
household	These days, most **households** have two or three TVs.
lose (one's) life	More than 20 people **lost their lives**, and many were injured.
mattress	There were not enough beds in the house, so they slept on an old **mattress** on the floor.
oxygen	For a fire to start, three things are needed: a spark, fuel and **oxygen**.
spark	A **spark** from a cigarette can easily start a fire.
spread	The wind was strong, so the flames **spread** quickly.
take to court	If you don't pay on time, they might **take you to court**.

Descriptive verbs SB page 22

1 ★☆☆ **Complete the sentences with the words from the list in the correct form.**

~~rage~~ | dive | scream | demolish
grab | flee | smash

0 The fire _raged_ through the house in minutes.

1 The woman was leaning out of the window. She _____ for help.

2 The man _____ into the river to rescue the boy.

3 The building was unsafe after the fire, so the council _____ it.

4 People _____ from the burning building.

5 The woman _____ her bag before she left the burning building.

6 The man _____ the window to rescue the boy from the fire.

2 ★★☆ **Complete the crossword with synonyms of the underlined words in the sentences. Use descriptive verbs.**

1 Together we <u>ran out of</u> the burning building.

2 The girl <u>broke</u> the bedroom window.

3 'Help me,' she <u>cried out</u>.

4 She <u>quickly took hold of</u> my hand.

5 Later, they <u>decided to destroy</u> the building because it was unsafe.

6 They don't know why the fire <u>started</u>.

7 The fire had been <u>burning</u> for three hours when they finally put it out.

8 People were <u>throwing themselves</u> into the nearby river and swimming across it.

Pronunciation

Initial consonant clusters with /s/
Go to page 118.

3 ★☆☆ **Unscramble the words about fire.**

1 a m e f l   _____

2 a r k s p   _____

3 g e n y o x   _____

4 e u f l   _____

5 a s t e r d i s   _____

6 a s c a p h t r o t e _____

4 ★★☆ **Complete the sentences about a fire with the correct form of the phrases in the list. Then number the sentences in the order the events happened.**

flames | spread | fight a fire | break out
catastrophe | lose your life

a [ ] The fire brigade worked hard, but sadly three people _____ in the fire.

b [1] It was late at night when the fire _broke out_.

c [ ] The firemen _____ bravely.

d [ ] The newspapers reported it as a _____ .

e [ ] It was a windy night so the flames _____ quickly before the fire brigade arrived.

f [ ] A man walking his dog saw the _____ and he called the fire brigade.

Time periods SB page 25

5 ★★☆ **Match the two sentence halves.**

1 In this day and age

2 A few decades ago

3 In the last century

4 In the Middle Ages

a not many people had colour TV.

b there were two world wars.

c there was no electricity.

d most people have a smart phone.

6 ★★★ **Write your own sentences using the time phrases.**

1 In this day and age _____

2 A few decades ago _____

3 In the last century _____

4 Nowadays _____

5 Not so long ago _____

6 In the Middle Ages _____

READING

1 REMEMBER AND CHECK **Read the sentences and mark them T (True) or F (False). Then check your answers in the article on page 21 of the Student's Book.**

1 The Great Fire of London started in a butcher's shop. ☐

2 The wind was blowing from the west. ☐

3 The fire started in a wealthy area of the city. ☐

4 Some people escaped by jumping into the river. ☐

5 Luckily, the wind changed direction. ☐

6 A lot of people lost their lives but not many buildings were destroyed. ☐

2 Look at the photo. Which century do you think the girl lived in? How old do you think she is?

3 Now read the autobiography and check your answers.

4 Scan the text and find three more words that show life was hard.

overcrowded _____ _____ _____

My name's Ellen and I grew up in Manchester in the 19th Century at the time of the Industrial Revolution. I was born in 1853, and at that time, Manchester had 108 cotton mills. It was called Cottonopolis.

Life wasn't easy for children in those days, and most children were dead by the age of five. Some might say they were the lucky ones because they didn't have to go to work in a mill.

By 1853, most people had moved from the countryside to the city for work, and the city was dirty and overcrowded. Three or four families often lived in the same house. We lived in one room in the basement of a house. It was damp, dark and cold and we only had one bed. The toilet was outside in the street, and we had to share it with all our neighbours. There wasn't any running water in the house

either. We didn't have any clean drinking water, and many people died from typhoid fever or cholera. My eldest brother died of typhoid two months before I was born. My family had only lived in the city for a year and my mother wanted to move back to the countryside. My father decided they should stay in the city.

I was eight when I started work at the cotton mill. The noise was terrible and the air was filled with white dust from the cotton. I couldn't breathe and I wanted to run away.

The mill was a dangerous place for children. I knew that. On my first day, a little boy died. He was sitting under the machines collecting all the waste when the accident happened. The managers were supposed to stop the machines for cleaning, but they never did. Why should they? Boys like him had very little value.

One morning, after I had been working there for a few months, I had a terrible accident too. I was very tired that morning. I had been working for three hours when, for just a second, I closed my eyes and that's when it happened. A woman grabbed me and pulled me away from the machine, but it was too late, I had lost three fingers on my right hand. At the time I was pleased. 'Now I don't have to work anymore,' I thought. But no, I was wrong. They found me another job – a job where I didn't need a hand.

5 Answer the questions.

1 Why was Manchester called Cottonopolis?

_____

2 How long had the family been living in Manchester when Ellen's brother died?

_____

3 Why did Ellen want to run away when she entered the mill?

_____

4 Where was the little boy working when he had the accident?

_____

5 How long had Ellen been working when she had her accident?

_____

6 What happened to Ellen?

GLOSSARY

Industrial Revolution the period of time during which work began to be done more by machines in factories than by hand at home

mill a factory where particular goods are produced

typhoid an infectious disease spread by dirty water and food

6 Do some internet research about your country. Find the answers to these questions and write a short paragraph.

1 Did children under the age of ten use to work in the 19th Century?

2 What kind of jobs did they use to do?

3 Do they still work in your country today?

4 What kind of jobs do they do now?

DEVELOPING WRITING

A newspaper article

1 Read the outline for writing a newspaper article. Match the information to the headings.

introduction | main body | conclusion | lead sentence | headline

1 _____ This paragraph answers the questions 'what?', 'where?', 'when?' and 'how?'

2 _____ This paragraph (or paragraphs) give more details and background information. Action verbs are used to make the article interesting and more dramatic.

3 _____ This is short and catches the reader's attention.

4 _____ This is usually a memorable sentence to end the article.

5 _____ This is usually a short opening sentence that summarises the article and answers the question 'who?'

2 Now read the article and label it 1–5 for the headings from Exercise 1.

31st AUGUST 1997

Tragedy in Paris

Princess Diana has died after a car crash.

Tragedy struck late last night, as Princess Diana left the Ritz Hotel with Dodi al-Fayed. They were travelling in a car across Paris when at 35 minutes after midnight, the car crashed in the Alma tunnel below the River Seine.

Photographers were chasing the car on motorbikes, and their driver was driving very fast. They crashed into the wall of the tunnel. French radio reported that a spokesperson for the royal family expressed anger with press photographers who relentlessly followed Princess Diana.

Dodi al-Fayed and the driver died at the scene. The Princess and her bodyguard were rushed to hospital in an ambulance in the early hours of Sunday morning. Her bodyguard, Trevor Rees-Jones, survived. Surgeons tried for two hours to save Diana's life but she died at 3 am.

This morning, the world woke up to the shocking news that Princess Diana was dead.

3 Now read the news story again and find the answers to the questions below. Write sentences.

1 Who?

2 What?

3 Where?

4 When?

5 How?

4 Write an article for the school newspaper about a dramatic event in your town. This can be true or something that you make up. Ask yourself the questions in Exercise 3 and use the answers to plan your article. Write about 200 words.

CHECKLIST ✔

- Use narrative tenses
- Follow the outline of an article
- Use action words
- Check spelling and punctuation

LISTENING

1 🔊 09 Listen to a conversation about schools in the 19th Century.
Which subjects did children use to have to study? (Circle) a, b or c.

a Maths, Reading and Writing   **b** Maths, Chemistry and Physics   **c** Reading, Writing and Geography

2 🔊 09 Listen again and match the sentence halves.

1	Before 1870, only boys	a	playgrounds for boys and girls.
2	After 1870, all children	b	at 5 pm.
3	They used to have separate	c	posters on the walls.
4	They didn't use to have any	d	used to go to school.
5	In the olden days, not many men	e	so they could walk home for lunch.
6	They didn't use to have Geography	f	used to become teachers.
7	They used to finish school	g	aged five to ten used to go to school.
8	They used to have a two-hour lunch break	h	lessons at school.

DIALOGUE

1 Put the lines in order to make a conversation between father and son.

- [ ] **DAD** No, the Millennium Bridge didn't use to be here either.
- [ ] **DAD** Yes, it did. It used to be an old power station.
- [1] **DAD** I used to walk along here every afternoon after school.
- [ ] **DAD** It's completely changed. The Globe Theatre didn't use to be here.
- [ ] **DAD** That's the Tate Modern. It's a big modern art gallery.
- [ ] **SON** And what's that huge building over there?
- [ ] **SON** Did it always use to look like that?
- [ ] **SON** Didn't it? What about this bridge?
- [ ] **SON** Lucky you, Dad! Has much changed?

2 Complete the mini dialogues with the phrases.

use to watch | your favourite meal
the other children | would play football
in those days | school dinners

1

TINA What did you use to do after school?

DAD I would meet up with _____ in the neighbourhood. If it was raining, we would play board games indoors. If the weather was fine, we _____ in the park.

2

DEAN What kind of programmes did you _____, Grandma?

GRAN I liked films, especially Hollywood musicals. I would watch all the old Fred Astaire and Ginger Rogers films. They weren't in colour though. They were all in black and white _____.

3

TONY Did you use to take a packed lunch to school, Mum?

MUM No, I didn't. We used to get _____. The menu was the same every week or every two weeks. I can still remember every single meal.

4

TONY What was _____?

MUM I can tell you my least favourite meal – a slice of beef, beetroot and mashed potato.

Speaking part 1

Exam guide: Interview

In the First speaking exam, there will be two examiners and two candidates in the room. You will have a conversation with one of the examiners (the interlocutor). The other examiner (the assessor) will just listen. You will be examined on your ability to talk naturally to the examiner. Part 1 will last for 1½ minutes.

- First the examiner will say:
  Good morning / afternoon / evening.
  My name is … and this is my colleague …
  And your names are?

- Then the examiner will ask you questions from certain categories, such as:
  1 People you know
  2 Things you like
  3 Places you go to

1 Match the questions to the categories above. Write the number.

1 What's your favourite subject at school? Why do you like it? `2`
2 Who are you most like in your family? Tell me about him / her. ☐
3 Do you like reading? What do you like to read? Why? ☐
4 Are there any nice places to go in your town? What are they? What makes them nice? ☐
5 Do you have a best friend? Tell me about him / her. ☐
6 Do you enjoy using the Internet in your free time? Why / Why not? ☐
7 Tell us about a good teacher you've had. ☐
8 Tell us about the things you like doing at the weekend. ☐
9 Where would you like to go for your next holiday? Why would you like to go there? ☐

Exam guide: Interview

- As well as answering the questions you need to give your opinions. For example:
  Do you like reading?
  Yes, I love reading. I've just finished a brilliant horror story called 'Anya's Ghost'.
- Keep your answers short but try to make them interesting.
- Ask the examiner to repeat the question if you need him / her to.
- Don't forget to speak clearly.

2 🔊 **10** Now listen to the interview with a candidate. How well did she do? Grade her performance. Give her 1 star for 'could do better', 2 stars for 'good' and 3 stars for 'excellent'.

1 She gives the correct responses. ★ ★★ ★★★
2 Her voice is clear. ★ ★★ ★★★
3 Her word and sentence stress are good. ★ ★★ ★★★
4 She talks fluently. ★ ★★ ★★★
5 She uses good vocabulary. ★ ★★ ★★★
6 She sounds natural. ★ ★★ ★★★

3 Imagine you are an exam candidate yourself. Answer the questions from Exercise 1 and ask a friend to listen to you and grade your performance.

CONSOLIDATION

LISTENING

1 🔊 11 **Listen and (circle) A, B or C.**

1   What does the girl not want to do when she leaves school?
   A   make plans
   B   start working
   C   go to university

2   The girl says she could work in a factory …
   A   if the money is good.
   B   for a short time.
   C   for a long time.

3   Why does the girl not want to be like her father?
   A   He works evenings and weekends.
   B   He doesn't like his job.
   C   He doesn't earn much money.

2 🔊 11 **Listen again and answer the questions.**

1   Why doesn't the girl want to go to university?

   _____

2   What does she say about jobs at the moment?

   _____

3   What kind of job does she want?

   _____

4   Why does she think working in a factory could be OK?

   _____

5   What does she think is good about a 9 to 5 job?

   _____

GRAMMAR

3 (Circle) **the correct options.**

1   I *go / 'm going* for a walk in the park every weekend.

2   Max and I *go / are going* for a walk tomorrow morning.

3   When I arrived, the place was empty – everyone *went / had gone* home.

4   I used to *going / go* and play by the river every day.

5   In the future, life *is being / will be* very different from today.

6   The film finished, so then I *had gone / went* to bed.

7   Tomorrow I'm *meeting / meet* my friends in town.

8   Many years ago, my family *would / used to* live in a very small flat.

VOCABULARY

4 **Complete the sentences with one word.**

1   In this _____ and age, almost everyone knows how to use a computer.

2   I've _____ a resolution to never eat chocolate again.

3   She only started work here last month, but she's already got _____ .

4   I want to travel – I don't want to get married and settle _____ .

5   Is this song from the 1970s or the 1980s? Well, it's a song from a few _____ ago, anyway.

6   He went to university and got a _____ in Mathematics.

7   The firemen _____ the fire for hours before they managed to put it out.

8   As you get older, it becomes harder to _____ your ways.

9   The house was old and dangerous so the city council _____ it.

10 The post office said it could take _____ to two weeks to deliver the package.

5 **Match the sentence halves.**

1   When he reached the age of 63 ☐
2   The fire broke out because ☐
3   The flames spread very quickly ☐
4   When she stopped working, ☐
5   They were very scared, ☐
6   She decided to start a career ☐
7   It isn't a good idea to form ☐
8   My friend didn't do very ☐
9   It's up to you. ☐
10 I was up late. ☐

a   to the next building.
b   well in the exam, unfortunately.
c   in banking.
d   That's why I'm tired.
e   he decided to retire from his job.
f   she took up photography.
g   You decide.
h   bad habits.
i   someone carelessly dropped a cigarette.
j   and they screamed very loudly.

DIALOGUE

6 **Complete the conversation with the phrases in the list.**

don't be silly | where shall I start
now you mention it | you're a star
stuff like that | here we go
where have you been hiding | what's up

JOHNNY   Hi, Sophie! I haven't seen you for ages.
1_____?

SOPHIE   Hi, Johnny. Yes, I'm sorry. I've just had so much to do these days.

JOHNNY   Oh 2_____ with the excuses. Like what?

SOPHIE   Oh, well, 3_____?
Like, revising for exams, taking care of my brother …

JOHNNY   Your brother? 4_____ with him?

SOPHIE   Didn't you hear? He had a pretty bad accident a few weeks ago. He was in hospital for over two weeks. He's home now. I have to look after him in the afternoon when I get back from school.

JOHNNY   Wow, Sophie. 5_____.
I don't know how you manage to look after someone who's ill.

SOPHIE   Oh, 6_____. There isn't much to manage really – but he can't move around much so I just have to get food and things, help him get dressed, 7_____. Anyway, he's my brother so I want to help him. I'm sure you've helped people in your family too.

JOHNNY   Well, 8_____, I helped to look after my dad when he was ill a few years ago.

SOPHIE   See? We all do things when we have to. And that's what I'm doing. It is tiring, though.

READING

7 **Read the text and mark the sentences T (true) or F (false).**

Charles Dickens and 'Hard Times'

Charles Dickens was one of the most famous and successful writers in England during the 19th Century. He became very wealthy and once travelled to the USA to give talks. His books are still popular today and many have been made into films – *Great Expectations*, *Oliver Twist* and *A Christmas Carol* are perhaps the best known examples.

But Dickens' life was not always an easy one, especially when he was a small boy. His parents had problems with money, and so in 1824 they sent young Charles, only just turned 12 years old, to work in a factory – he had to stick labels onto bottles full of 'blacking', a polish for cleaning shoes. He was paid six shillings a week – that's about £12.50 a week in today's money. He hated the place.

A short time later, his father was sent to prison because he owed money – this happened to many people at that time. Then the family house was sold, and Charles' mother, brothers and sisters went to live in the prison too. Charles never forgot this period of his life. As an adult, he wanted people to know about the terrible conditions that children often had to work in. And when he started writing, his stories were full of people who suffered the things that he had gone through himself. In fact, one of his novels is called *Hard Times*.

1 There are film versions of some of Charles Dickens' novels. ☐

2 Charles' parents sent him to the factory because they needed money. ☐

3 Charles was almost 13 when he went to work in the factory. ☐

4 Charles' work was to polish shoes. ☐

5 Charles went to live in a prison with his family. ☐

6 In his later life, Charles wanted to help improve the situation for children. ☐

WRITING

8 **Write a short paragraph (100–120 words). Imagine you are 12-year-old Charles Dickens, working in the factory. Say what your work is like and how you feel.**

3 | WHAT'S IN A NAME?

GRAMMAR

(don't) have to / ought to / should(n't) / must   SB page 32

1 ★☆☆ **Complete the sentences with the phrases in the list.**

go and see it | go to bed so late | buy a hairbrush | wear something warmer | be so shy | ask someone

1 You should _____

2 He shouldn't _____

3 I must _____

4 I shouldn't _____

5 We ought to _____

6 We must _____

2 ★★☆ **Circle the correct options.**

1 It's a holiday tomorrow. We *have to / don't have to* go to school.
2 Well, it's your party. You *have to / don't have to* invite people you don't like.
3 Coffee isn't free here. You *have to / don't have to* pay for it.
4 Just your surname is OK. You *have to / don't have to* write your full name.
5 Well, those are the rules – you *have to / don't have to* be sixteen to be allowed in.

3 ★★☆ **Complete with *have to / has to / don't have to / doesn't have to*.**

TOM Why do I ¹_____ go to bed now? Sally ²_____ , and she's only two years older than me.

DAD That's right. But Sally ³_____ get up at seven o'clock to go to school. You do.

TOM Only because you say so. It only takes me fifteen minutes to get dressed and have breakfast.

MUM But you ⁴_____ have a shower too, remember.

TOM OK, twenty minutes. But I ⁵_____ leave the house until 7.50. So, I could get up at 7.30. And so, I ⁶_____ go to bed now.

MUM All right, but remember – it's me who ⁷_____ deal with you when you're tired and irritable in the morning!

4 ★★★ **Complete using a form of *have to* and a suitable verb.**

1 I'm going to a wedding tomorrow so no T-shirt!
   I _____ a suit and tie.
2 Josh, if you're going skateboarding, you _____ in the park and not go on the road.
3 He can't come out with us tonight – he _____ his baby brother.
4 In some countries you can eat with your hands – you _____ with a knife and fork.
5 Her parents are rich, so she _____ about money.
6 Well if you want better grades, you _____ more.
7 We _____ the dishes – we can put them all in the dishwasher.
8 My sister and I have each got a computer now, so we _____ one any more.

had better (not) `SB page 33`

5 ★☆☆ **Match the sentence halves.**

1 We mustn't be late, so ☐
2 This food might not be good anymore, so ☐
3 We've already spent a lot of money, so ☐
4 It's probably going to be cold, so ☐
5 My eyes are getting tired, so ☐
6 I didn't really understand that, so ☐
7 I think the water's dirty in that tap, so ☐
8 I hate it when you call me names, so ☐

a I'd better wear a jumper.
b we'd better leave now.
c I'd better read it again.
d we'd better not drink it.
e you'd better throw it away.
f you'd better not do it again.
g we'd better not buy anything else.
h I'd better not look at a screen any more.

6 ★★☆ **Use 'd better / 'd better not and a verb from the list to complete each sentence.**

apologise | call | eat | study
stay | tell | turn | wear

1 A We've got a test tomorrow.
  B Well, you _____ tonight, then.
2 A My parents get worried if I get home late.
  B OK, we _____ too long at the party, then.
3 A I think he's quite angry about what I said.
  B You _____ , then.
4 A I've got tickets for the concert tonight.
  B Well, you _____ Steve. He couldn't get one so he'd be envious.
5 A I don't feel too well.
  B Well, you _____ any more crisps, then.
6 A Look! That man's fallen over. I think he's ill.
  B We _____ an ambulance right away.
7 A The neighbours are complaining about the noise.
  B Oh, OK. We _____ the music down a bit.
8 A It's a very special party tomorrow night.
  B Yes, I know. We _____ something nice.

can('t) / must(n't) `SB page 35`

7 ★☆☆ **Complete what each of these signs means. Use can / can't or mustn't and a verb where necessary.**

1 You _____ turn right.
2 You _____ park here.

3 You _____ go in here.
4 You _____ take photos here.

5 You _____ here.
6 You _____
_____ .

GET IT RIGHT! 👁

Confusion between could and should

Learners sometimes confuse could and should.

We use should to indicate that it's a good idea or that it's what will happen under normal circumstances. On the other hand, we use could to indicate that something may be true or possible.

✓ If you want, you **could** bring some drinks.
✗ If you want, you ~~should~~ bring some drinks.

Circle the correct modal verb.

0 Two hours (should) / could be enough to do everything. That's how long it normally takes.
1 I would like to ask if I should / could have another month to finish the project.
2 If you want to get healthier, you should / could eat balanced meals.
3 On the other hand, there should / could be risks with that plan.
4 Should / Could you please consider my application and look at my case?
5 I think that we should / could choose the route around Lake Frene.
6 Maria did not know whether she should / could tell the police or not.

VOCABULARY

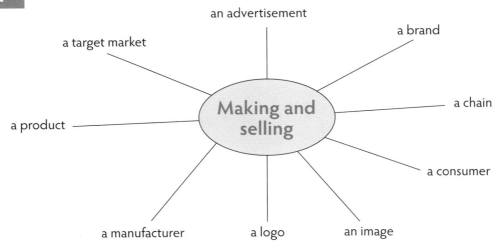

Making and selling

- an advertisement
- a brand
- a chain
- a consumer
- an image
- a logo
- a manufacturer
- a product
- a target market

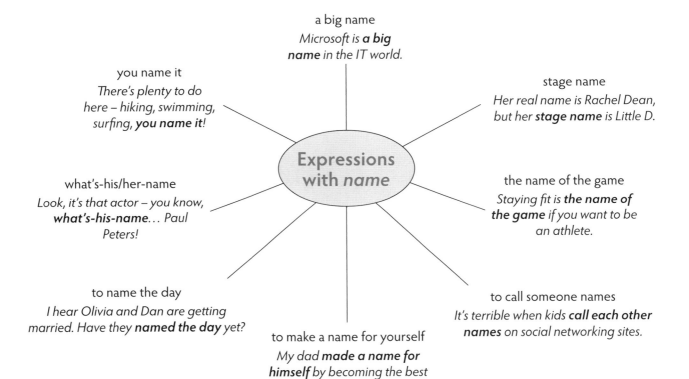

Expressions with *name*

a big name
*Microsoft is **a big name** in the IT world.*

stage name
*Her real name is Rachel Dean, but her **stage name** is Little D.*

you name it
*There's plenty to do here – hiking, swimming, surfing, **you name it**!*

the name of the game
*Staying fit is **the name of the game** if you want to be an athlete.*

what's-his/her-name
*Look, it's that actor – you know, **what's-his-name**… Paul Peters!*

to call someone names
*It's terrible when kids **call each other names** on social networking sites.*

to name the day
*I hear Olivia and Dan are getting married. Have they **named the day** yet?*

to make a name for yourself
*My dad **made a name for himself** by becoming the best in the business.*

Key words in context

approved	The **approved** uniform at our school is grey trousers and a white shirt.
blend in	The colour of the animal's skin helps it to **blend in** with its surroundings.
distinguish	It's important to **distinguish** between work and play.
had better	If we want to pass the exam, I think we**'d better** do some revision.
household name	Prince William is a **household name** in the UK.
impact	She said some wonderful things that had a big **impact** on us.
make a fool of (someone)	I said a really stupid thing – I think I **made a fool of myself**!
memorable	It was a **memorable** day – I'll never forget it.
permission	My mum didn't give me **permission** to use her car.
unique	It's the only one in the world – it's completely **unique**.

Making and selling SB page 32

1 ★★☆ **Complete the phrases with the words in the list.**

product | image | logo | manufacturer | consumer
target market | brand | advertisement | chain

1 a _____ of shops

2 a _____ of things like doors and windows

3 the _____ that a company makes

4 an _____ in a magazine or on TV

5 the _____ that a company tries to sell to

6 the _____ that people prefer to buy

7 the _____ that a company uses to identify itself

8 an _____ that a company shows to the public

9 a _____ who buys goods or services

2 ★★☆ **Circle the correct options.**

1 This shop is one of a *brand / chain* – there are over 30 in this country.

2 I love that company's new TV *logo / advertisement*.

3 Some of the best-known car *manufacturers / products* are Korean.

4 The marketing department designed a new *image / logo* to put on their products.

5 Our company is launching a new *target market / product* next week.

6 Many companies support a charity – it improves their *consumer / image*.

Pronunciation

Strong and weak forms: /ɒv/ and /əv/

Go to page 118.

Expressions with *name* SB page 35

3 ★★☆ **Complete with an appropriate expression.**

1 I eat everything – _____, I'll eat it!

2 Nobody knew him ten years ago, but he soon _____ for himself as an actor.

3 They're engaged to be married but they haven't _____ yet.

4 You've probably never heard of Peter Gene Hernandez, but his _____ is Bruno Mars.

5 Go and talk to that boy – um, _____, you know, the new guy.

6 Well if you want to play, you have to train too – sorry but that's _____.

7 It's so childish, I think, when kids at school _____ other kids _____.

8 Everyone knows who she is – she's a _____ in this country!

4 ★★☆ **Complete the crossword.**

1 → 'Monkey' is not an … name in Denmark.

1 ↓ I want to sell my laptop, so I'm going to put an … in the school magazine.

2 You need your parents' … to go on the school trip.

3 The girl tried to … in with her new friends by listening to the same music as them.

4 It's a very expensive car – the … market is super rich people.

5 I won my first prize today, so it's a … day for me!

6 The company puts its …, a big tick, on all of its shoes.

7 Their advertising had a big … on young people.

8 It's one of a … of 120 shops all over the country.

9 The company is trying to improve its … .

10 This isn't my usual … of toothpaste.

11 All you do is buy things – you're a real …, aren't you?

5 ★★★ **Answer the questions.**

1 What was the most memorable day of your life?

2 What is your favourite brand of clothes? Why?

3 Can you name a song, or film, that has had a big impact on you? What impact did it have?

4 Have you (or anyone you know) got something that is unique? What is it?

5 Who is the biggest name in sport in your country?

6 What is the best chain of shops in your country?

READING

1 REMEMBER AND CHECK **Match the phrases from columns A, B and C to make sentences. Then check your answers in the blog entry on page 31 of the Student's Book.**

A	B	C
1 Companies really want to find	given to a car	on an English expression.
2 A brand name should be	especially important	and easy to understand.
3 The name 'WhatsApp'	a name for their product	of the whole product package.
4 'Nova' was the name	but it's an important part	that they don't need to change later.
5 Brand names are	unique, easy to remember	that didn't work in Spain.
6 A brand name isn't everything,	is based	for the teenage market.

2 **Read the blog quickly. Which of the three titles is the best one?**

A People's names aren't easy to remember.

B Why do we sometimes forget people's names?

C Why can't I remember things?

FORUMS   MEMBERS   BLOGS   GALLERY

Hi, Paul here. OK, I'm sure this has happened to you too, right? Last weekend ^{1}_____ , chatting to some friends, and my friend Hannah introduces me to this girl, who seems nice and starts talking to me. And then some music comes on and I think: 'Wow, this is cool music' and I want to ask the girl to dance – and then I realise I have no idea what her name is. Hannah told me but – it's gone. And I'm too embarrassed to ask her again. So I ^{2}_____ and go somewhere else. Ridiculous, right?

Anyway, this morning I Googled 'remembering names' and there was an article that said that if you don't remember someone's name, ^{3}_____ you don't have a good memory – it's because you don't care. That if you're not motivated to remember, then you won't. Well I'm not so sure. I mean, the girl was nice so I was sort of motivated to remember her name, ^{4}_____ . And here's another thing the article said: 'Some people ^{5}_____ in their own memories.' They say, 'I'm not good at learning names.' It says people don't remember because they think they're not good at it.

I don't know. What do you guys out there think?

Greg178: No, I disagree. The reason you don't remember people's names is that you're immediately focussed on what they're saying. You don't repeat their name over and over in your head – well, ^{6}_____ . Unless, of course, you're more interested in their name than what they have to say.

VVXX: Sounds right to me. Sometimes I meet people and I know I'll never see them again, so I don't even try to remember their name. But if I think a person looks cool or ^{7}_____ , then I remember.

JaneGH: It's not that I don't care what a new person's name is, it's just that I'm busy learning other things about them. I'm so busy ^{8}_____ their face that I forget to listen for their name. But all I've got to do then is ask them!

3 **Read the blog again. Put these phrases into the correct places (1–8).**

1 but I got distracted
2 don't have much confidence
3 make an excuse
4 taking in
5 it's not because
6 I'm at this party
7 not at a party, anyway
8 might be important

4 **Read the blog again. Mark the sentences T (true) or F (false).**

1 Paul met a girl called Hannah at a party. ☐
2 Paul found an article about remembering names in a magazine. ☐
3 Paul isn't sure if what the article said is true. ☐
4 Greg178 thinks what someone is saying is more important than their name. ☐
5 VVXX always tries to remember a new person's name. ☐
6 JaneGH concentrates more on someone's face than on their name. ☐

DEVELOPING WRITING

An email about rules

1 **Read the email. What does Burcu want to know about?**

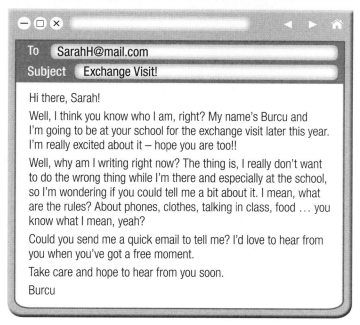

To SarahH@mail.com

Subject Exchange Visit!

Hi there, Sarah!

Well, I think you know who I am, right? My name's Burcu and I'm going to be at your school for the exchange visit later this year. I'm really excited about it – hope you are too!!

Well, why am I writing right now? The thing is, I really don't want to do the wrong thing while I'm there and especially at the school, so I'm wondering if you could tell me a bit about it. I mean, what are the rules? About phones, clothes, talking in class, food … you know what I mean, yeah?

Could you send me a quick email to tell me? I'd love to hear from you when you've got a free moment.

Take care and hope to hear from you soon.

Burcu

2 **Now read Sarah's email in reply. Answer the questions that follow it.**

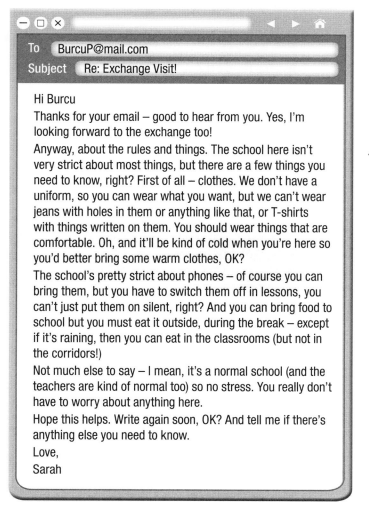

To BurcuP@mail.com

Subject Re: Exchange Visit!

Hi Burcu

Thanks for your email – good to hear from you. Yes, I'm looking forward to the exchange too!

Anyway, about the rules and things. The school here isn't very strict about most things, but there are a few things you need to know, right? First of all – clothes. We don't have a uniform, so you can wear what you want, but we can't wear jeans with holes in them or anything like that, or T-shirts with things written on them. You should wear things that are comfortable. Oh, and it'll be kind of cold when you're here so you'd better bring some warm clothes, OK?

The school's pretty strict about phones – of course you can bring them, but you have to switch them off in lessons, you can't just put them on silent, right? And you can bring food to school but you must eat it outside, during the break – except if it's raining, then you can eat in the classrooms (but not in the corridors!)

Not much else to say – I mean, it's a normal school (and the teachers are kind of normal too) so no stress. You really don't have to worry about anything here.

Hope this helps. Write again soon, OK? And tell me if there's anything else you need to know.

Love,

Sarah

1 Which of the things Burcu asks about does Sarah not mention?

2 What are students not allowed to wear at Sarah's school?

3 What advice does Sarah give Burcu about clothes?

4 What do students have to do with their phones when they go into the classroom?

5 Where are students not allowed to eat at Sarah's school?

3 **Answer the questions about Sarah's email. They are all about writing informally.**

She writes: 'you'd better bring some warm clothes, OK?'

1 She uses the word 'OK' to
check for understanding / show disagreement.

2 What word does she sometimes use instead of 'OK'?

She writes: 'it'll be kind of cold when you're here.'

3 'kind of' means *very / a bit.*

4 Find and underline another time when she writes 'kind of' in the email.

She writes: 'good to hear from you.'

5 She has left out the words *This is / It is.*

6 Find two other times when she leaves words out. What are these words?

4 **Imagine that Burcu wrote her email to you. Write a reply to her.**

a Think about the rules in your school and the things Burcu asks about:

- clothes
- food
- phones
- talking in class

b What other rules (if any) should she know about?

c This is an informal email (like Sarah's) – think about how you can make it easy for Burcu to read.

Write about 200–250 words.

CHECKLIST ✔

Include a greeting

Use informal language

Respond to all questions

Sign off the email

LISTENING

1 🔊 **13 Listen to a conversation between Annie, Ben and the new girl. Circle the correct answers.**

1 The new girl's name is …
  A Maureen.   B Morgan.   C Morwenna.

2 She is from …
  A Cornwall.   B Wales.   C London.

3 Some places where she's from …
  A have nothing to do there.
  B have names with strange pronunciation.
  C aren't very nice.

2 🔊 **13 Listen again and mark the statements T (true) or F (false).**

1 Annie doesn't understand Morwenna's name. ☐

2 The name 'Morwenna' is Welsh. ☐

3 A part of Morwenna's family lives in Cornwall. ☐

4 Morwenna says Newquay is a good place for surfing. ☐

5 The water in Newquay is warm. ☐

6 Ben pronounces Mousehole correctly. ☐

7 People in Cornwall don't mind if names are pronounced wrongly. ☐

8 Annie gets Morwenna's name wrong. ☐

3 🔊 **13 Listen again. Complete these parts of the conversation.**

1

ANNIE	I've never been there. Cornwall, I mean.
MORWENNA	Oh, ¹_____ It's really nice. We go quite often – my mum's got family down there. In Penzance.
BEN	Anything to do there?
MORWENNA	Sure – there are nice beaches and if you like surfing, ²_____ Newquay.
ANNIE	But isn't the water really cold?
MORWENNA	Well, yes! So if you go surfing, ³_____ a wetsuit, to keep warm in the water.

2

MORWENNA	Really. If you go, ⁴_____ how to pronounce the names. Local people don't like it when tourists say the names wrong.
ANNIE	I guess not.
BEN	I think Annie's right – ⁵_____ a new brain.
MORWENNA	Sorry?
BEN	Oh, nothing. Listen, ⁶_____ back, the next lesson starts in a few minutes.

DIALOGUE

1 Put the phrases into the correct places.

'd better take | should know
should visit | 'd better learn

1

A You live in Vancouver, don't you? I've always wanted to go there.

B That's right. And if you ever go there, you ¹_____ Stanley Park. It's beautiful!

A Is the weather nice there?

B Well, it can be OK in summer – but it rains quite a lot, so you ²_____ an umbrella!

2

A You live in Hamburg, right? I've always wanted to go there.

B Yes, I do. If you come to my city, you should go and see the Miniature Wonderland. It's fantastic.

A Do you think I ³_____ German before I go?

B Well, you ⁴_____ a few words, I guess – but lots of people speak English, so you don't have to worry too much.

2 Write a dialogue between you and a friend.

The friend begins:

'You live in (name of your town / city), right? I've always wanted to go there.'

Give the friend some advice about where to go, what to see and what to do.

Use the dialogues in Exercise 1 to help you.

Listening part 1

1 🔊 **14** You will hear people talking in four different situations. For questions 1–4, choose the best answer (A, B or C).

1 You hear a man in a shop.

What is the problem with the shoes?

A His wife doesn't like them.

B He doesn't think they're right for him.

C They're too small for him.

2 You hear a girl talking about her hobby, sudoku puzzles.

What does she say about them?

A The puzzles are always easy to do.

B She always solves the puzzles.

C They develop her thinking abilities.

3 You hear a man talking about his trip to China.

Which cities did he visit?

A Beijing, Shanghai and Chengdu

B Beijing, Shanghai and Xi'an

C Beijing, Chengdu and Xi'an

4 You hear a woman talking about getting to and from work.

How does she travel?

A by car

B by plane

C by bus

Exam guide: multiple choice

In part 1 of the First listening exam, you hear eight extracts – they are not connected to each other. You hear each extract twice.

For each extract there is a short statement saying what you're going to hear. Then there is one question. You have to choose the best answer from three options (A, B or C).

- Read the questions and options in advance. It's important to get a clear idea of what you have to decide.
- The first time you hear the monologue, try to remove, if possible, at least one of the answers. Then, the second time you listen, you can concentrate on getting the correct answer.

- The speaker won't always give you a direct answer. Instead, you will have to infer the answer – for example, we can infer 'She is a writer' is the correct answer when we hear 'She spends all day at her computer, typing out her ideas.'
- Remember that you will hear things that are intended to distract you from the correct answer, so avoid making quick decisions.

2 🔊 **15** You will hear people talking in four different situations. For questions 1–4, choose the best answer (A, B or C).

1 You hear a teenage schoolgirl.

Why did she change schools?

A Her old school was too far away.

B She wanted to work harder.

C The new school is cheaper.

2 You hear part of a radio interview with a man.

What does he do?

A He writes the words for possible songs.

B He is a songwriter and singer.

C He takes pieces of music and writes words for them.

3 You hear a woman talking about her hobby, birdwatching.

How does she feel while she is birdwatching?

A bored

B hopeful

C calm

4 You hear a boy who wants to be a chef.

Why did he first become interested in cooking?

A He ate some good Italian food.

B He enjoyed cooking dinner for himself.

C His mum cooked a fantastic dinner for his birthday.

4 DILEMMAS

GRAMMAR
First and second conditional (review)
`SB page 40`

1 ★☆☆ **Match the sentences with the pictures.**

1 If we lose this game, I won't be happy.
2 If we lost this game, I'd be very surprised.
3 If it snows tomorrow, we won't have to go to school.
4 If it snowed here, it would be very strange.

2 ★★☆ **Complete the sentences with the verbs in brackets to make first or second conditional sentences.**

0 I *will tell* (tell) you my secret if you ___*promise*___ (promise) not to tell anyone.

1 Be careful. The cat _____ (bite) you if you _____ (touch) it.

2 If he _____ (be) taller, he _____ (be) a really good basketball player.

3 If I _____ (meet) the President, I _____ (ask) him to do more for the environment.

4 Hurry up. If we _____ (not leave) now, we _____ (miss) the train.

5 If I _____ (know) the answer, I still _____ (not help) you.

6 If we _____ (not stop) talking now, the teacher _____ (get) angry with us.

7 I _____ (run) away if I _____ (see) a tiger in the jungle.

8 Our team is the best. I _____ (be) very surprised if we _____ (not win).

3 ★★☆ **Complete the sentences with the verbs in brackets to make second conditional sentences.**

What [1]_____ you _____ (do) if you found an envelope full of money in the street? [2]_____ you _____ (take) it to the police station? Or [3]_____ you _____ (keep) it and buy yourself something you really wanted? [4]_____ you _____ (buy) your mum and dad a present? If you [5]_____ (buy) them a present they [6]_____ (want) to know where you got the money from. If you [7]_____ (tell) them the truth maybe they [8]_____ (not be) so happy. And if you [9]_____ (not tell) them the truth, you [10]_____ (feel) really bad. You know what, I hope I never find an envelope full of money in the street!

Time conjunctions `SB page 40`

4 ★☆☆ ⟨Circle⟩ **the correct words.**

1 Dad's going to get a new computer *when / unless* he has enough money.

2 I'll phone you *until / as soon as* she leaves.

3 We'll start the meeting *until / when* Mr Benson arrives.

4 *If / Until* I don't pass my English test, I'll take it again.

5 You won't pass your driving test *if / unless* you practise more.

6 We'll watch the game *as soon as / until* half time.

5 ★★☆ **Complete the sentences with *if, unless, until* or *as soon as*.**

1 _____ we hurry up, we'll be late for the party.

2 Jim's got the tickets so we'll have to wait _____ he gets there before we can get in.

3 What will you do _____ we don't get any homework this weekend?

4 She can't talk because she's in the shower. She'll call you _____ she gets out.

5 I'm seeing John tonight so I'll ask him _____ I see him.

6 _____ we can't get tickets, we can just watch the game on TV at my house.

7 I've got to go to the shops. Can you look after Tim _____ I get back?

8 I can't go to the party _____ I finish my project by Friday.

wish and *if only* SB page 41

6 ★☆☆ ⟨Circle⟩ the correct word.

1 My dad wishes he *has / had* more time.

2 Paula wishes she *can / could* go to the game tonight.

3 If only the neighbour's dog *won't / wouldn't* bark all day.

4 The teacher wishes her students *weren't / aren't* so noisy.

5 If only I *am / was* taller.

6 Liam wishes Lucy *will / would* talk to him.

7 If only I *could / can* play the piano.

7 ★★☆ Read the sentences. What does Julia wish?

0 'My sister keeps taking my clothes.'

I wish my sister wouldn't keep taking my clothes.

1 'I don't understand Maths.'

If only _____

2 'The boys in my class are so childish.'

I wish _____

3 'I can't find my phone. Where is it?'

I wish _____

4 'I can't afford to buy those new shoes.'

If only _____

5 'I want to stay in bed but I've got to get up for school.'

I wish _____

6 'I've got too much homework this weekend.'

If only _____

Third conditional (review) SB page 42

8 ★☆☆ Match the sentence halves.

1 I wouldn't have gone to the concert ☐

2 I would have got a much better mark ☐

3 We would have saved a lot of money ☐

4 She would have got completely lost ☐

5 If you hadn't kicked the ball so hard, ☐

6 If she had apologised, ☐

7 If I had had his number, ☐

8 If they'd been a bit quieter, ☐

a if I'd studied harder.

b if she hadn't had a map.

c it wouldn't have knocked my glasses off.

d I would have phoned him.

e if I had known it was going to be so bad.

f they wouldn't have woken the baby.

g I would have forgiven her.

h if we'd eaten at home.

9 ★★☆ Read and complete the sentences with the verbs in brackets. Use either the positive or negative form.

My friend Dave threw a pencil and it hit the teacher. The teacher was angry. Dave didn't say anything. The teacher thought it was me and gave me detention. I went to detention and met a girl called Sara. I asked her over to my place and she said 'yes'. Now Sara's my best friend.

0 If Dave *hadn't thrown* a pencil, it *wouldn't have hit* the teacher. (throw / hit)

1 If he _____ honest, he _____ to detention. (be / go)

2 If I _____ to detention, I _____ Sara. (go / meet)

3 If I _____ Sara, I _____ invite her to my house. (meet / be able to)

4 If she _____ 'no' to my invitation, I _____ at home alone. (say / stay)

5 If she _____ to my place, we _____ best friends. (come / become)

GET IT RIGHT!

would have + past participle

Learners sometimes underuse *would have* + past participle, or use it in the *if*-clause where the past perfect tense is required.

✓ After the musical, we **would have gone** to a restaurant but we didn't have time.

✗ After the musical, we ~~would go~~ to a restaurant but we didn't have time.

✓ We would have appreciated it if you **had contacted** us.

✗ We would have appreciated it if you ~~would have contacted~~ us.

Circle the correct tense of the verb.

1 If I *would have to / had to* choose between the two schools, I would choose the larger one.

2 I *would have liked / 'd like* to visit, but I didn't have the chance.

3 It would have been better if there *would have been / had been* more jobs available.

4 The food wasn't as tasty as I *would have liked / 'd like*.

5 If I'd known about the risks, I *wouldn't have taken / wouldn't take* part.

6 We could have learned more if the facilities *would have been / had been* better.

VOCABULARY

Being honest

bad	**good**	*now*
get away with (something)	do the right thing	now (for the present)
hide the truth	be open about (something)	now that
tell a lie	tell the truth	now and again
cheat	own up (to something)	just now
		now (for near future)

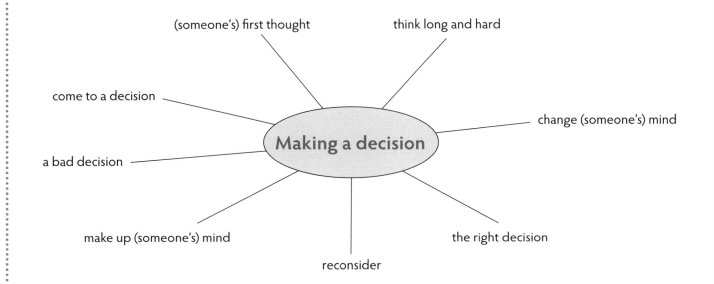

(someone's) first thought · think long and hard · come to a decision · change (someone's) mind · **Making a decision** · a bad decision · make up (someone's) mind · reconsider · the right decision

Key words in context

as soon as	I'll phone you **as soon as** I know.
go-karting	Many F1 drivers start their careers **go-karting**.
helmet	You should always wear a **helmet** when you cycle to protect your head.
if	**If** you don't slow down, we're going to have an accident.
if only	**If only** I had a better computer. This one is so slow.
race	He won the **race** by more than 30 seconds.
reunite	The twins were separated when they were two years old and only **reunited** 20 years later.
unless	I won't say anything **unless** he asks me.
until	We waited **until** 10 pm and then went home.
when	**When** I got home there was no one there.
wish	It's such a beautiful day I **wish** I didn't have to work.

Being honest SB page 40

1 ★★☆ **Match the sentence halves.**

1 Why don't you just own ☐
2 I want to tell him the ☐
3 I can be very open ☐
4 I always find it really difficult to tell ☐
5 It's not always easy to do ☐
6 There's no point trying to hide ☐
7 She believed me! I never thought I'd get ☐
8 Liam's always trying to cheat ☐

a with my mum. We have a great relationship.
b the truth. People always find out.
c a lie. My face just goes bright red.
d away with that lie.
e in exams. He tries to look at my paper.
f the right thing, so thank you for being honest.
g up and tell her you broke her phone?
h truth but it's just so hard.

2 ★★☆ **Complete the dialogue with the words in the list. There is one extra word.**

truth | open | do | Hide | Own | cheat | lie | get

MANDY   So what do you think we should do?
        ¹_____ up and tell the ²_____ ?
RACHEL No way. She'll kill us. I think we have to tell
        a ³_____ and say it wasn't us.
MANDY   We'll never ⁴_____ away with it. I think
        we have to ⁵_____ the right thing.
RACHEL Which is?
MANDY   Be ⁶_____ about it. Say we were hungry
        and there was nothing else to eat.
RACHEL But it was her birthday cake! She won't
        accept that as an excuse.
MANDY   So what do you think we should do?
RACHEL ⁷_____ the truth. Say the dog ate it.
MANDY   The dog? That's brilliant! Why didn't you
        suggest that earlier?

Making a decision SB page 43

3 ★★☆ **Match the expressions and the definitions.**

1 first thought ☐
2 to think long and hard ☐
3 to change your mind ☐
4 to reconsider ☐
5 to make up your mind ☐
6 a bad decision ☐

a to really consider something
b to think about your decision again
c to come to a decision
d not the right decision
e to come to a different decision
f original idea

4 ★★★ **Answer the questions.**

1 What were your first thoughts when you met your best friend?

_____

2 What is the best decision you have ever made?

_____

3 What is the worst decision you have ever made?

_____

4 When do you find it difficult to make up your mind?

_____

5 Can you remember a time when you changed your mind about something? What was it?

_____

6 What kind of things do you have to think long and hard about?

_____

WordWise SB page 45

now

5 ★★☆ **Rewrite the sentences with *now* in the correct place.**

1 I go and see the local team play and again but I'm not a huge fan.

_____

2 John left just so if you run, you'll catch him.

_____

3 We hardly ever see Lewis that he's got his own phone.

_____

4 We've missed the bus. What are we going to do?

_____

READING

1 REMEMBER AND CHECK Put the events in the order that they happened. Then check your answers in the story on page 42 of the Student's Book.

- ☐ He receives money that helps him change his life.
- ☐ He remembers advice his grandfather once gave him.
- ☐ He meets Sarah.
- ☐ He sees his sisters for the first time in 16 years.

- ☐ He finds a ring in his cup.
- ☐ Billy hears a sound that is a little unusual.
- ☐ He refuses money that would help change his life.
- ☐ He shows the ring to an expert.
- ☐ He returns the ring to its rightful owner.

2 Read the article. What was the dilemma the game show contestants faced?

Golden Balls

A few years ago there was a game show on TV in which the contestants faced a really difficult dilemma. I can't really remember what happened in the show, I just remember how it finished. At the end there were two contestants and they had the chance to win some money. Depending on how successful they'd been during the show, the amount of money could be anything from a few hundred pounds to well over £50,000. To get their hands on this money, they had to make one final decision.

In front of each of them were two balls which opened. One had the word 'split' written inside, the other had the word 'steal'. If they wanted to share the money, they chose the 'split' ball. If they wanted to keep all the money for themselves, they chose the 'steal' ball. Each player chose a ball and then they showed it to each other at exactly the same time.

But it wasn't quite so simple. If they both chose the 'split' ball, then they each went home with half the money. If one player chose the 'split' ball while the other chose the 'steal' ball, then the one who'd stolen went home with all the money, leaving the other player with no money at all. However, if they both chose the 'steal' ball, then neither of them got any money at all.

Before they chose the ball, both players had a few minutes to tell the other one what they were going to do.

Of course, they always promised they'd share but they weren't always telling the truth. I remember always feeling really happy when the two players kept their promises and they both went home with some money. It's always good to see the best side of people. But unfortunately it didn't always end that way and when one player stole from the other it made me feel really bad, especially when there was a lot of money involved. However, I think the best feeling I had was when two greedy players both stole. It was great to see the look of disappointment on their faces when they realised they'd both thrown away the money.

The programme showed all sides of human nature, the good and the ugly. It only lasted for a few years and then they stopped making it. I think that was probably a good thing.

● posted 19/07/15 | 1,425 views | SHARE

---

3 Read the article again and answer the questions.

There are two players, Sam and Jim. There is a total prize money of £10,000.

How much does each player win in the situations below? How does the writer feel watching it?

1 They both choose the 'split' ball.   Sam £_____   Jim £_____   Writer feels _____

2 They both choose the 'steal' ball.   Sam £_____   Jim £_____   Writer feels _____

3 Jim chooses 'split', Sam chooses 'steal'.   Sam £_____   Jim £_____   Writer feels _____

4 Jim chooses 'steal', Sam chooses 'split'.   Sam £_____   Jim £_____   Writer feels _____

4 Imagine you are a contestant in the show. There is £10,000 to win. What would you do and why? Write a short paragraph.

DEVELOPING WRITING

A diary entry about a dilemma

1 Read the diary entry. What is Olivia's dilemma and what does she decide to do?

I have a confession. I've not shown my best friend the trust she deserves and I'm feeling really bad about it. It all started when she asked to borrow my tablet to check her email. Of course, I let her use it. [A] The problem is that she forgot to close it afterwards so when I went online a few hours later, her email page was the first thing I saw. I went to close it down when I noticed an email, a very unusual email. [B] but there it was — an email from my boyfriend to my best friend and the title was my name — 'Olivia!' I thought [1]_____. I knew I should just close the page but I had to know: why was he writing to her? I didn't even know he had her email address. I knew it was the [2]_____ to do but I opened the message. [C] As soon as I read it I knew I'd made a horrible mistake. The message was all about arranging a surprise party for my birthday at the end of the month.

Now I've got a horrible dilemma. Should I [3]_____ and [4]_____ or say nothing and [5]_____ from her? If I was braver, I'd tell her what I'd done. [D] I think that this time I won't say anything and pretend that the party is a surprise. But I know there's one thing I'll never do again — I'll never let anyone use my tablet to check their email!

2 Complete the text with the phrases in the list. There is one extra phrase.

long and hard | tell a lie | tell her the truth | own up | wrong thing | hide the truth

3 These sentences have all been removed from the diary entry. Complete them using the verbs in brackets to make second or third conditionals. Then decide in which of the spaces A–D they go.

1 If I _____ (can turn) back time, I _____ (close) the page without taking a look. ☐
2 If I _____ (not see) it, I _____ (never think) of reading any of her messages. ☐
3 If I _____ (tell) her, she _____ (never speak) to me again. ☐
4 If I _____ just _____ (say) 'no', I _____ (not have) this dilemma. ☐

4 Read the dilemmas and then complete the conditional sentences.

1 *I broke my best friend's games console.*

a If I'd been more careful,

_____

b If he knew it was me,

_____

2 *I saw my best friend cheating in an exam.*

a If I told the teacher,

_____

b If she had studied harder,

_____

3 *My friend wants to borrow £100 from me. It's all the money I've got.*

a If I gave it to him and he never paid me back,

_____

b If he had been more careful with his money,

_____

5 Choose one of the dilemmas in Exercise 4 (or think of one of your own) and write a diary entry of about 250 words.

- Explain the dilemma.
- Explain the background behind the dilemma.
- Talk about what you should do.

CHECKLIST ✔

☐ Conditional sentences
☐ Honesty vocabulary
☐ Explanation of dilemma
☐ Background to dilemma
☐ Thoughts about what you should do

LISTENING

1 🔊 **16** Listen to the conversations. Match them with the pictures.

2 🔊 **16** Listen again and complete these parts of the conversations.

Conversation 1

TEACHER   Is there anything you'd like to tell me?

LIAM   I d_____ k_____ w_____ to s_____

TEACHER   You know this is a very serious offence.

LIAM   I know, Sir. I'm so a_____ .

Conversation 2

WOMAN   My dress!

MAN   Oh I'm s_____ s_____ .

WOMAN   It's OK. It's only water.

MAN   I know but it was so clumsy of me.

WOMAN   D_____ w_____ a_____ it. Really, it's nothing.

Conversation 3

TINA   But I haven't got you a present or even a card. I f_____ a_____ a_____ it.

LUCY   No w_____ . It's fine.

DIALOGUE

1 Put the dialogue in the correct order.

1	TINA	Tell me it's not your birthday today.
	TINA	It's not fine. I'm going straight out and getting you something nice.
	TINA	But I haven't got you a present or even a card. I feel awful about it.
	TINA	What are you doing?
	TINA	And tonight I'm taking you out for a meal. No argument.
13	TINA	Oh. I see.
	TINA	And I've forgotten it. I'm so embarrassed.
	LUCY	Don't be so silly. It's easily done.
	LUCY	No seriously. You don't need to.
	LUCY	It is. It's the big one – 40.
	LUCY	No worries. It's fine.
	LUCY	But I can't. I've kind of got plans already.
	LUCY	Well, it's just me and a few friends going out dancing.

PHRASES FOR FLUENCY   SB page 45

1 Complete the phrases with the missing vowels.

1 _r_ y_ _ _ _t _f y_ _r m_nd?

2 b_l_ _v_ _t _r n_t

3 b_tw_ _n y_ _ _nd m_

4 _ w_s w_nd_r_ng _f

5 _ny ch_nc_?

6 wh_t's w_th

2 Complete the conversations with the phrases from Exercise 1.

1 A _____ the grumpy face, Ben? Life's not so bad, is it?

   B No, I'm just a bit tired. I didn't get a lot of sleep last night.

2 A I think we should take a break and go and play some tennis.

   B _____ , I was thinking exactly the same thing!

3 A Um, Jen, I don't know if you're busy tonight but _____ you'd like to go to the cinema with me?

   B Like to? I'd love to!

4 A We've got visitors and the living room's a mess. It needs tidying – Jack, _____

   B Sorry, Mum, but I'm busy playing Minecraft.

5 A That dog's really cute. I think we should take it home with us.

   B _____ It probably belongs to someone.

6 A Are you going to Yolanda's party?

   B _____ , I don't really want to go so I think I might make up an excuse and give it a miss.

Pronunciation

Consonant–vowel word linking
Go to page 119.

Writing part 2

1 Look at the task. <u>Underline</u> the most important information in it.

 WE ARE LOOKING FOR STORIES FOR A NEW WEBSITE FOR TEENAGERS.

Your story must start with the following sentence:
I opened the suitcase and could hardly believe my eyes — it was more money than I had ever seen in my life.

Your story must include:

- A decision
- A police officer

Write your story in 140–190 words.

2 Read Alan's answer. What two parts of the question does he fail to answer?

I opened the suitcase and could hardly believe my eyes – it was more money than I had ever seen in my life. I closed it quickly and put the case back onto the seat. I was excited but I was also nervous – very nervous. I sat down next to it and thought about how this case had fallen into my hands.

The woman had seemed normal. We'd started chatting, first about the weather and then about where we were going. She was on her way to visit her aunt. A man dressed in a dark suit passed by our carriage. Her mood changed immediately. She seemed anxious and didn't want to talk. Then she got up suddenly. She asked me to look after the case and left. Two hours later the train had reached its final stop, the station where I was getting off. What was I going to do? Leave the money on the train or take it with me? I counted the money when I got home: £500,000 exactly. I used it to open a small shop. Now, more than twenty years later I have about fifty supermarkets across the whole country. I often think about that woman.

3 Look at the notes Alan made before he wrote his story. Use his story to answer the questions he asked himself.

1 Where was I?

2 Why did I have this suitcase?

3 How did I feel when I saw the money?

4 What did I decide to do?

5 What were the consequences?

Exam guide: writing a story

In part 2 you have to answer one of four questions. You have a choice of an article, a review, an essay, an email/letter or a story. It must be 140–190 words.

- Read the question carefully. Underline the important information. Keep within the word limit. The starting sentence doesn't count in this total.
- Think carefully about who your reader is and why you are writing.
- Use the first sentence given to spark your imagination. Ask yourself questions like *who*, *why*, *where* and *what next*.
- Think carefully about what kind of language you will use. When you write a story, you need to show a good use of the narrative tenses.
- Use descriptive language. Think carefully about the verbs, adjectives and adverbs you use.
- Think about how you are going to link the sequence of events. Words like *as soon as*, *then*, *after that*, *before*, *after*, etc. will help you do this.

4 Read the task. Plan and then write your answer.

 **WE ARE LOOKING FOR STORIES FOR AN ENGLISH LANGUAGE MAGAZINE FOR TEENAGERS.**

Your story must start with the following sentence:
Should I stay or should I go? I had 30 seconds to decide.

Your story must include:

- A dilemma
- A bike

Write your story in 140–190 words.

5 Ask a friend to read your story and complete the sentences about it.

I really like the …

I thought the story was …

The language you used well was …

You could improve it by …

CONSOLIDATION

LISTENING

1 🔊 **19 Listen and (circle) A, B or C.**

1 The girl doesn't want the T-shirt because …
   A it's too big.
   B she doesn't like the colour.
   C she doesn't like the name on it.

2 The girl wants to change the T-shirt for …
   A a belt.
   B a different T-shirt.
   C two other T-shirts.

3 The man suggests that the girl could …
   A keep the T-shirt.
   B give the T-shirt to her brother.
   C give the T-shirt to someone else.

2 🔊 **19 Listen again and mark the sentences T (true) or F (false).**

1 The girl doesn't like clothes with the names of companies on. ☐

2 All the clothes in the shop have the company name on. ☐

3 The T-shirt was a present from the girl's brother. ☐

4 The shirt has a hole in it. ☐

5 The girl hasn't got the receipt. ☐

6 The belt is more expensive than the T-shirt. ☐

7 The girl is bigger than her friend Jenny. ☐

8 She decides to give the T-shirt to her friend. ☐

VOCABULARY

3 Match the sentences.

1 Everyone knows who she is. ☐
2 She's travelled all over the world. ☐
3 She's totally honest. ☐
4 She just doesn't know what to do. ☐
5 She stuck with her original decision. ☐
6 She doesn't want to use her real name. ☐

a She can't make up her mind at all.
b She didn't want to change her mind.
c So she's decided to use a stage name.
d She's a big name in this country.
e I've never heard her tell a lie.
f You name it, she's been there!

4 (Circle) the correct options.

1 I haven't decided yet – I'm going to think long and *hard / strong* about it.

2 We don't go there very often – just *now that / now and again*.

3 Come on, tell us the *lie / truth* about what happened.

4 I know you did it. Come on, you should just *get away with it / own up to it*.

5 I really don't care if people *make me / call me* names.

6 I think you've made the wrong decision. If you want to *reconsider / come to a decision*, please call me.

7 I don't like the *logo / brand* of this company. It's not very well designed.

8 He's the owner of a big *chain / brand* of shops in the north of the country.

GRAMMAR

5 Correct the sentences.

1 I wish you are here.
   _____

2 I was happier if the weather was better.
   _____

3 If only I know the answer to this question.
   _____

4 We'd better to leave now, I think.
   _____

5 I'll phone you when I'll get home.
   _____

6 Do you think we should asking for some help?
   _____

7 He's a great guitar player – if only he can sing better.
   _____

8 If he'd left earlier, he hadn't missed the start of the film.
   _____

9 The bus ride there is free, so you have to pay for it.
   _____

10 Let's wait as soon as 5 pm to call them.
   _____

DIALOGUE

6 **Complete the dialogue with the phrases in the list.**

I was wondering | any chance
are you out of your mind | had better
should have been | believe it or not
what's with | between you and me

MANDY Hey, Jim. ¹_____
if you're going to Lucy's party later.

JIM Yeah, I'm going. Why?

MANDY ²_____ I can go
with you? I just don't like arriving
at parties on my own.

JIM Sure, no problem.

MANDY That's great. Thanks. Hey, you'll
never guess what happened to
me in a shop this morning.

JIM Tell me. What happened?

MANDY Well, I bought a really cool shirt for
the party tonight.
³_____ , it was
£79.99! I can't believe I spent so
much!

JIM Wow, that's really expensive. But
so what?

MANDY Well, you know, my parents gave
me some money for my birthday, so
I paid cash with two £50 notes. I put
them on the counter, and,
⁴_____ , the
woman put the change on top of
the notes! I picked it all up and left.
So I got the shirt and my money
and the change! How cool is that?

JIM Cool? ⁵_____ ?
It's dishonest. Think about the poor
shop assistant – she'll probably have
to pay that money out of her own
pocket. You ⁶_____
take it back and explain. Say it was
a mistake.

MANDY No way. She
⁷_____ more
careful.

JIM Whatever. I'm sure you wouldn't
like it to happen to you.

MANDY Oh come on, Jim.
⁸_____ you?
Don't be so boring.

JIM Boring? Mandy, what you did was
stealing, you know?

SPAM

Back in 1937 there was a company in the USA that made a kind of meat that was in a can. The story goes that they had a competition amongst the people who worked there to give this canned meat a name. The winner won $100 for inventing the name: Spam. (Some people think this means 'Specially Processed American Meat). Spam became very popular during World War II in Britain, when it was a very important food item. Spam is still made and sold today around the world.

But interesting things have happened to the name. In the 1970s there was a famous comedy programme on British TV which did a sketch about a café where everything on the menu had Spam in it. They even invented a song which is mainly the word 'Spam' sung over and over again.

Now, when they did this, the comedians created the idea that Spam was everywhere, that you couldn't avoid it and no one really wanted it. And then, more than twenty years later when emails began, people started receiving lots of unwanted emails – they were everywhere and you couldn't avoid them. And what is that kind of email called? Why, spam, of course.

The company that makes Spam (the meat, that is) was not too happy about this use of the name and tried for many years to find a way to stop it. But finally they gave up. Now Spam is both things, and sales of the meat haven't suffered much – in 2007, the seven billionth can of Spam was sold.

READING

7 **Read the online article. Answer the questions.**

1 What is the possible reason for the name 'Spam' for canned meat?

_____

2 When and where was Spam an important food?

_____

3 What idea did the comedy programme create about Spam?

_____

4 Why is unwanted email called 'spam'?

_____

5 How did the meat manufacturer feel about emails being called 'spam'?

_____

6 How many cans of Spam had been sold by 2007?

_____

WRITING

8 **Think of two products you know – one that you like the name of, and one that you don't like the name of. Write a paragraph (100–120 words). Include this information:**

- what the products are and what they do
- what their names are
- why you like / dislike the names (the sound? the meaning of the name? the way the name is written? another reason?)

5 | WHAT A STORY!

GRAMMAR
Relative pronouns `SB page 50`

1 ★☆☆ **Complete the sentences with *who, whose, where* or *which*.**

1 The book _____ I have just read is called *Clockwork Angel*.

2 It is a fantasy novel _____ was written by Cassandra Clare.

3 The name of the girl _____ is the heroine of the novel is Tessa Gray.

4 The story is set in London, _____ all the action takes place.

5 Tessa Gray is looking for her brother, _____ has disappeared.

6 Tessa gets help from two friends _____ names are Will and Jem.

Defining and non-defining relative clauses `SB page 50`

2 ★★☆ **Combine the sentences about a famous vampire with *who, which, where* or *whose*.**

0 Abhartach was a vampire. He came from Ireland.
   Abhartach was a vampire who came from Ireland.

1 It was a legend. It inspired Bram Stoker to write *Dracula*.
   _____

2 Abhartach was an evil magician. He had very strong powers.
   _____

3 He lived in Derry. He ruled a small kingdom.
   _____

4 He was an evil ruler. His people were afraid of him.
   _____

5 *Dracula* comes from an Irish word. It means bad blood.
   _____

3 ★★☆ **Complete the conversation with *which, who, that, where* or *whose*.**

HOLLY What kind of books do you like reading?

ANNA I like reading books [1]_____ have vampires or witches in them. My favourite book is one about a girl [2]_____ grandmother was a witch. It's a historical novel [3]_____ is about a witch.

HOLLY Is it set in England?

ANNA No, it's set in America, [4]_____ Mary, 'the witch girl', is sent after her grandmother's death. What about you? What kind of books do you like?

HOLLY I like historical novels. I'm reading one now [5]_____ is set in Victorian England. It's about a poor girl [6]_____ has to work. She works for a famous medium, Madam Savoya, [7]_____ job is to contact the spirits of dead people for their relatives.

ANNA It sounds like the kind of book [8]_____ I'd like to read. Can I borrow it when you've finished?

4 ★★☆ **Put the words in the correct order to make sentences with non-defining relative clauses.**

1 daughter, / My / lives / in / Madrid, / who / an / author / is
   _____

2 film, / The / stars / Helen Weaver, / which / out / on / DVD / is / now
   _____

3 storyteller, / The / work / all / over / the / world, / whose / takes / him / in / Japan / is / at / moment / the
   _____

4 Prague, / where / boy / the / story / the / in / grew up, / my / hometown / is
   _____

5 heroine / story, / the / of / The / whose / father / French, / is / called / Sophie / is
   _____

5 ★★☆ Write D (defining) or ND (non-defining) next to the relative clauses.

1 My favourite book, which is about a vampire, has now been made into a film. ☐

2 The boy, who had read the book, liked the film. ☐

3 The man who she's interviewing wrote the book. ☐

4 I couldn't find any travel literature on Morocco, where I'm going on holiday next month. ☐

5 My aunt, who is a poet, lives in London. ☐

6 The girl whose father was rescued in the story was Spanish. ☐

7 The fairy story, which was written in the 19th Century, is still read today. ☐

8 I couldn't watch the horror film which was on TV last night. ☐

6 ★★★ Rewrite the sentences with *who*, *which*, *where* or *whose* and the clauses in brackets.

0 The girl had long red hair. (mother is the heroine of the story)
The girl, whose mother is the heroine of the story, had long red hair.

1 The city is my home town. (all the action took place)

_____

2 The park is the scene of the crime. (the murdered woman's body was found)

_____

3 The story is very sad. (is set in a future world)

_____

4 The villain was in fact a good man. (was killed at the end of the story)

_____

5 The crime was never solved. (was committed at the beginning of the story)

_____

Relative clauses with *which* SB page 53

7 ★★☆ Read the sentence pairs. Write a new (third) sentence so that it has the same meaning as the sentence pair. Use *which*.

0 My parents used to read lots of stories to me when I was a child. I enjoyed this a lot.
My parents used to read lots of stories to me when I was a child, which I enjoyed a lot.

1 Their train arrived four hours late. This meant they missed the show.

_____

2 None of my friends had studied for the test. This made their parents really angry.

_____

3 My friend reads ten books a month. I find this amazing.

_____

4 Most of my friends don't like the new Tarantino film. I can't understand this.

_____

8 ★★★ Complete the sentences so they are true for you.

1 One of my friends _____, which is very good news.

2 Lots of people in my street _____, which I find annoying.

3 Not many people want to _____, which I find a great pity.

GET IT RIGHT! 👁

that vs. *which* in relative clauses

Learners sometimes mistakenly use *that* in non-defining relative clauses.

We can use *which* or *that* in defining relative clauses.

✓ This is the solution **that** you are looking for.

✓ This is the solution **which** you are looking for.

We only use *which* in non-defining relative clauses.

✓ I'm in Brazil, **which** is a beautiful country.

✗ I'm in Brazil, ~~that~~ is a beautiful country.

Tick (✓) the sentences which can use *that* or *which*.
Cross (✗) the sentences where only *which* is possible.

1 I spent £100, (which / that) is too much. ☐

2 I want a car (which / that) can go fast. ☐

3 Pete has a computer (which / that) has some good games on it. ☐

4 We should buy the one (which / that) is cheaper. ☐

5 I won't be there, (which / that) is a problem. ☐

VOCABULARY

Word list

Types of story

science fiction novel

crime novel

historical novel

poetry

horror story

travel literature

autobiography

romantic novel

short stories

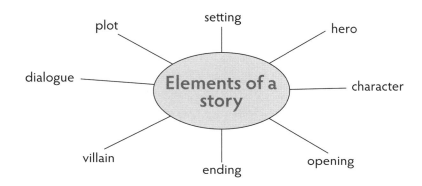

plot

setting

hero

dialogue

Elements of a story

character

villain

ending

opening

Key words in context

adolescent	The programme aims to encourage young **adolescents** to read more books.
anecdote	I love listening to **anecdotes** which people tell about travelling.
blockbuster	This movie will become a **blockbuster**; I'm sure it will make more money than *Avatar*.
capture (one's) attention	The story was so dramatic, it **captured everyone's attention**.
engage	If a book doesn't **engage** my interest from the beginning, I usually don't finish reading it.
fairy tale	I loved listening to **fairy tales** when I was a child.
influential	This theory has been **influential** for many years.
inspiration	She is a great teacher and has been an **inspiration** for a lot of students.
memorise	When my parents went to school, they frequently had to **memorise** long texts.
original	The **original** story comes from Africa, I believe.
pass down	This story has been **passed down** from generation to generation.
potential	This is a great book; it has the **potential** to be turned into a film.
revisit	Have you ever **revisited** the stories from your childhood?
romance	The **romance** between the main characters grows throughout the book.
special effects	I thought the film wasn't great, but the **special effects** were awesome.
tradition	Ireland is a country with a rich **tradition** in storytelling.

Types of story SB page 51

1 ★☆☆ **Match the descriptions of the books to their genres.**

1 poetry ☐
2 horror story ☐
3 short stories ☐
4 autobiography ☐
5 romantic novel ☐
6 historical novel ☐
7 travel literature ☐
8 crime novel ☐
9 science fiction ☐

a *War Horse* by Michael Morpurgo is set during World War I. Albert's father sells his horse Joey to the army and he goes into battle in France.

b In *Noughts and Crosses* by Malorie Blackman, Sephy is a cross and Callum is a nought. They fall in love, but in their world, noughts and crosses shouldn't be friends. Like Romeo and Juliet, their love is forbidden.

c *Jump Ball: A Basketball Season in Poems* by Mel Glenn. Through a series of poems we get to know the members of a school basketball team.

d *Fahrenheit 451* by Ray Bradbury is about a future world where books are not allowed. All books are burnt by 'firemen' whose job it is to start fires.

e *The Boy Who Biked the World* is by a cyclist, Alastair Humphreys, who completed a cycle trip round the world in four years. The story follows a boy's cycle trip through Europe and all the way through Africa.

f *Boy: Tales of Childhood* by Roald Dahl is about the author's childhood in Norway and his time at an English boarding school.

g *Haunted* by R.L. Stine is about a girl who is visited by a ghost from the future. Together they try to stop the death of a boy from occurring. Sometimes it's quite scary.

h *Whodunit? Detective Stories*, chosen by Philip Pullman, is a collection of detective stories by famous authors.

i *The London Eye Mystery* by Siobhan Dowd. Ted and Kat's cousin Salim gets on the London Eye. He never gets off again. Ted and Kat follow the clues across London to help the police to find their cousin.

Elements of a story SB page 53

2 ★★☆ **Complete the dialogue with the words in the list.**

characters | ending | villain | plot | setting | hero

HARRY OK, ask me questions and try to guess the book I'm thinking of.

MIKE Right. Where does the action take place?

HARRY The ^{1}_____ for the story is London in Victorian England.

MIKE What's it about?

HARRY The ^{2}_____ follows the life of one man in the past, the present and the future. The ^{3}_____ of the book is a very mean man, but he sees his faults and he changes. Three of the ^{4}_____ are ghosts.

MIKE Who's the bad character then? Who's the ^{5}_____ ?

HARRY There isn't one.

MIKE And does it have a happy ^{6}_____ ?

HARRY Yes, it does.

MIKE I think it's *A Christmas Carol* by Charles Dickens.

HARRY Well guessed. You're right. Now your turn.

3 ★★★ **Now complete the dialogue about a story (or a film) that you like.**

MIKE Where does the action take place?

ME The _____ for the story is _____ .

MIKE What's it about?

ME The _____ .

MIKE Who is the hero or heroine of the book?

ME _____ .

MIKE Who's the bad character then? Who's the _____ ?

ME _____ .

MIKE And does it have a happy _____ ?

ME _____ .

MIKE I think it's _____ by _____ .

4 ★★☆ **Complete the sentences with the words in the list.**

blockbuster | influential | tradition
romance | anecdotes | special effects

1 Nelson Mandela's _____ book, *A Long Walk to Freedom*, made people aware of the inequalities between people.

2 The two main characters fall in love, and the film follows their _____ .

3 My friend tells lots of funny _____ about her family.

4 The novel, which was very successful, was made into a _____ film.

5 It was a science fiction story, so the film had lots of amazing _____ .

6 Our family has a _____ of telling stories on Christmas Day.

READING

1 [REMEMBER AND CHECK] **Answer the questions. Then check your answers in the article on page 49 of the Student's Book.**

1 What does the writer say most people think of when they hear the word 'storytelling'?

_____

2 What forms of storytelling are mentioned?

_____

3 How did the Neanderthal man in the story die?

_____

4 What else do stories do other than just entertain us?

_____

5 How did storytellers find new stories?

_____

6 What do our stories reflect?

_____

2 **Read the article quickly. What is the profession of the 'star' in the picture? Circle the answer.**

A singer   B actor   C author   D politician

3 **Read the article again. Mark the sentences T (true) or F (false). Then correct the false sentences.**

1 Charles Dickens toured England and Europe as a storyteller. ☐

_____

2 Charles Dickens lived nearly two hundred years ago. ☐

_____

3 He earned a lot of money for his first performance of *A Christmas Carol*. ☐

_____

4 In those days, a lot of people couldn't read. ☐

_____

5 His family wanted him to stop touring because his readings weren't popular. ☐

_____

6 The carriage that Charles Dickens was in fell down a steep slope. ☐

_____

7 After the accident, Charles Dickens was scared of travelling by train. ☐

_____

8 Charles Dickens died of a heart attack in 1870. ☐

_____

A star is born!

Thousands of people came to the theatres and concert halls to hear him. Performances were sold out in Britain and America. People fainted at his shows. Who do you think he was? Well, he wasn't a pop star. He was in fact a writer, and he didn't live in this century. He lived nearly two hundred years ago. Maybe you have heard of him or read one of his books? His name was Charles Dickens.

In the 19th Century, Charles Dickens went on long tours in Britain and America. At each performance he read and acted out passages from his novels. These reading tours were very popular and they brought him fame and fortune.

Why did he go on tour with his books? His first tour was for charity – he wasn't paid for it. The first performance was of *A Christmas Carol* for 2,000 poor people in Birmingham. Many people in the audience couldn't read and so storytelling was very important to them. After this first performance, he was offered money to perform his readings at other places. At first he refused, but later he agreed to do more shows. He loved performing, and as a young man, he had wanted to be an actor. His tour of America from December 1867 to April 1868 earned him over £19,000, which was a huge amount of money at the time. It was a lot more than he earned from selling his books.

Charles Dickens' tours were very hard work as he travelled long distances by train, and trains were very slow in those days. His family and friends became worried about his health. They wanted him to stop touring.

In 1865, there was a terrible train crash at Staplehurst in Kent. All the carriages except one fell down a steep slope. What happened to Charles Dickens? He was in the one carriage that didn't fall down. After the accident, Charles Dickens was frightened of travelling by train, but he still continued his tours. His readings continued to be successful.

However, his friends and families were right to be worried about his health. Five years later, in 1870, Charles Dickens died of a stroke.

He is still very popular today and millions of people around the world read his books.

4 **If you could watch any 'star' perform live, who would that be? Write a short paragraph and give reasons for your choice.**

DEVELOPING WRITING

A book review

1 Match the sentence halves.

1 The hero or heroine of the book ☐
2 The setting ☐
3 The opening sentence ☐
4 It is very important to have a strong ending ☐
5 Some writers include jokes and witty dialogue ☐
6 There may be several different characters ☐

a at the beginning of the book is very important.

b which makes the story more entertaining.

c which satisfies the reader.

d is the person who is the main character.

e is where the action takes place.

f who have different strengths and weaknesses.

2 Look at the book cover. What genre of story is it?
(Circle) the answer.

A horror story   B travel adventure   C poetry
D romantic novel   E science fiction

3 Answer the questions about the book review.

Paragraph 1

1 What is the story about in general? (Write about the plot. But don't give the whole plot or the ending away.)

_____

_____

2 Where does the story take place? (Give the setting.)

_____

Paragraph 2

3 What happened to Tom, the main character, that the writer can identify with?

_____

_____

4 Did the writer like the book? What was his / her favourite thing about it?

_____

Paragraph 3

5 Does the writer recommend the book to older readers, younger readers or all ages?

_____

6 How does the reader rate the book? What are his / her reasons?

_____

_____

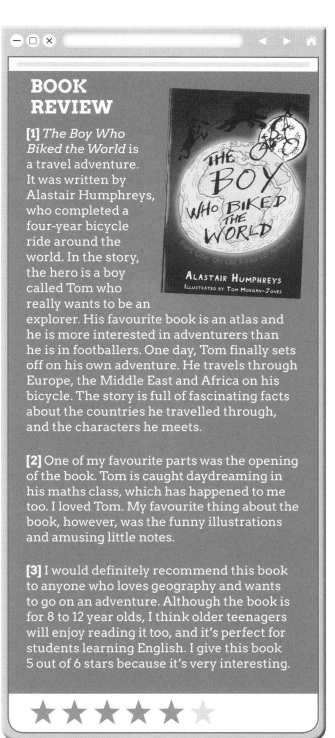

BOOK REVIEW

[1] *The Boy Who Biked the World* is a travel adventure. It was written by Alastair Humphreys, who completed a four-year bicycle ride around the world. In the story, the hero is a boy called Tom who really wants to be an explorer. His favourite book is an atlas and he is more interested in adventurers than he is in footballers. One day, Tom finally sets off on his own adventure. He travels through Europe, the Middle East and Africa on his bicycle. The story is full of fascinating facts about the countries he travelled through, and the characters he meets.

[2] One of my favourite parts was the opening of the book. Tom is caught daydreaming in his maths class, which has happened to me too. I loved Tom. My favourite thing about the book, however, was the funny illustrations and amusing little notes.

[3] I would definitely recommend this book to anyone who loves geography and wants to go on an adventure. Although the book is for 8 to 12 year olds, I think older teenagers will enjoy reading it too, and it's perfect for students learning English. I give this book 5 out of 6 stars because it's very interesting.

★ ★ ★ ★ ★ ☆

4 Now choose a book to review. Use the review and the questions above to help you to plan your writing. Then write a short review of the book in 200 words.

CHECKLIST ✔

☐ Use adjectives to make your review more interesting

☐ Use *which, who, whose* and *where* to improve your writing style

LISTENING

1 🔊20 **Read the sentences below. Then listen and write the numbers of the conversations (1, 2 or 3).**

a He sees three footballers who play for his favourite football team. ☐

b She sees a famous actor whose name she has forgotten. ☐

c She sees a friend of a friend that she hasn't seen for months. ☐

d He was in a restaurant, where he was having a meal with his parents. ☐

e She was in a bookshop, where she was buying a book for her brother. ☐

f She was shopping on Oxford Street. ☐

2 🔊20 **Listen again and mark the sentences T (true) or F (false).**

1 Katie saw her best friend in the bookshop. ☐

2 Amanda sometimes thinks of somebody and then they phone or text her. ☐

3 Jake's team won the football match on Saturday. ☐

4 Jake saw three Manchester United footballers in a restaurant. ☐

5 Sarah was shopping in Oxford Street when she saw the famous actor. ☐

6 The annoying thing is that Sarah can't remember the actor's address. ☐

DIALOGUE

1 Put the words in order.

1 never / what / believe / You'll / happened

_____

2 strangest / me / to / happened / thing / The

_____

3 me / finish / Let

_____

4 the / That's / annoying / thing

_____

5 the / are / chances / What

_____ ?

6 strange / What's / that / about

_____ ?

2 Put the dialogue in the correct order.

☐ MIKE Well, I haven't seen her for ages, but yesterday I was thinking about her – and then this morning I saw her. What are the chances, eh?

☐ MIKE Yes. And that's the annoying thing – you're always right!

1 MIKE The strangest thing happened to me this morning. I saw that girl Louise in town!

☐ MIKE Yes, she does but …

☐ SANDY Let me finish. And she works in a shop in town, too. So it isn't strange at all. Am I right?

☐ SANDY You saw Louise? What's strange about that?

☐ SANDY The chances are really good, actually. I mean, she lives here, doesn't she? And …

3 Complete the conversation with a word from the list. There is one extra word.

annoying | believe | chances | finish
happened | strange | strangest

MARIA You'll never ¹_____ what happened last night. That film *Ghost* was on TV! It was just the ²_____ thing!

PAUL Why? What's ³_____ about that? They show *Ghost* a lot on TV.

MARIA Let me ⁴_____. You see, I wanted to watch it on Sunday. I found the DVD at home, but the ⁵_____ thing was that it didn't work anymore.

PAUL Yes, I hate it when a DVD stops working properly.

MARIA But then the next day, I switched the TV on – and there it was! What are the ⁶_____ of that?

PAUL That is a little strange.

Pronunciation
The schwa /ə/ in word endings
Go to page 119. 🔊

Reading and Use of English part 5

Exam guide: multiple choice

In this part of the exam you will read a text followed by six multiple-choice questions. Each correct answer receives two marks.

- Read the whole text before looking at the questions.
- Read all the questions and leave the ones you are least sure about until the end.
- When you have finished the easy questions, go back to any questions you are unsure about. Ask yourself, 'Which answer is it not?' Eliminate the wrong or impossible answers first.

1 **You are going to read a review of Jules Verne's classic novel** *Around the World in 80 Days.* **For questions 1–6, choose the answer (A, B, C or D) which you think fits best according to the text.**

Jules Verne's novel, *Around the World in 80 Days,* has inspired many people to travel around the world in unusual ways. It has also inspired several films, TV series, theatre productions and even a board game.

So where did Jules Verne get the idea from? Jules Verne told a reporter that he had been sitting in a café in Paris one day when he saw a newspaper advertisement for the first ever tourist trip around the world in 1872.

In Jules Verne's story, a wealthy English gentleman, Phileas Fogg, accepts a bet of £20,000 that he can travel round the world in 80 days. Phileas Fogg is a man who is very hard to please. For example, he fires his servant because he brings him some water to wash in that is 29°C instead of 30°C. He has a very strict routine and he follows it to the letter every day.

Fogg employs a new servant, Passepartout, and on Wednesday, 2nd October, 1872, they set off on the journey round the world. While he's in India, Fogg falls in love with an Indian girl, Aouda. The journey ends back in London with Fogg believing that he has arrived a day too late and that he has lost the bet. He tells Aouda that he cannot marry her now, as he's too poor. Passepartout learns that they have got the date wrong. The party travelled eastward, so they gained a day. Fogg hurries to his club and arrives there in time to win the bet and the story ends happily.

The story is an easy read. The humorous twists and turns of the plot keep you entertained throughout. It is a romantic adventure story that I would strongly recommend to all my friends.

1 What does the reviewer explain in the first paragraph?
   A The story inspired people of Phileas Fogg's generation to travel.
   B The story has given people the idea of trying to travel around the world in different ways.
   C The story has inspired adventurers around the world to draw maps of their travels.
   D The story has inspired adventurers to navigate ships around the world.

2 What gave Jules Verne the idea for the story?
   A He had just returned from an interesting trip around the world.
   B He had seen a film about a trip around the world.
   C He had seen a play at the theatre about a round-the-world holiday.
   D He saw an advertisement for a holiday trip around the world.

3 What does the reviewer mean by: 'he follows it to the letter'?
   A Phileas Fogg writes a letter about his routine every day.
   B He follows a routine written down in a letter.
   C He has written the routine down in a letter for his valet.
   D He follows exactly the same routine every day.

4 Why does Phileas Fogg employ a new servant?
   A His old servant boils the water to too high a temperature for his wash.
   B His old servant makes one little mistake.
   C His old servant is always making mistakes.
   D His new servant charges less money.

5 Why can't Phileas Fogg marry Aouda?
   A He has fallen in love with another girl.
   B He is already married.
   C He thinks he doesn't have enough money to marry.
   D He thinks he has lost the bet so he has to set off on another journey.

6 What is the reviewer's opinion of the book?
   A The book is a fun adventure story with romance that everybody will enjoy reading.
   B The book is only entertaining for people who like romance novels.
   C The book has a very serious message about world travel for readers of all ages.
   D The reviewer recommends that you read the book before setting out on a long journey.

6 | HOW DO THEY DO IT?

GRAMMAR
Present and past passive (review)
SB page 58

1 ★☆☆ (Circle) the correct option.

1 The best sports cars *make / are made* in Italy.
2 The concert *showed / was shown* live on TV.
3 She *texts / is texted* me at least five times a day.
4 The 2012 Olympics *held / were held* in London.
5 My dad *makes / is made* model trains as a hobby.
6 Letters *deliver / aren't delivered* on Sundays.
7 Jacob's really good at tennis. He *coaches / is coached* by his mum.
8 A 63-year-old woman *won / was won* the talent show.

2 ★★☆ Complete with the past passive forms of the verbs in brackets.

The school magic show was a complete success. All the tickets ⁰ *were sold* (sell) and some amazing tricks ¹_____ (perform) by three very talented magicians. Here are some of my favourites: The headmaster ²_____ (saw) in half. A piece of paper ³_____ (turn) into hundreds of butterflies. Loads of gold coins ⁴_____ (find) behind the ears of Adam from 6E. And of course, a rabbit ⁵_____ (pull) out of a hat.

3 ★★★ Write questions in the present or past passive using the prompts.

0 President Kennedy / shoot
   When was President Kennedy shot?
1 America / discover by Columbus
   When _____
2 the first helicopter / build
   When _____
3 BMW / make
   Where _____
4 The Oscars / hold
   Where _____
5 2014 World Cup final / play
   Where _____

4 ★★★ Write answers to the questions in Exercise 3. Use the clues in the list to help you.

Germany | Rio de Janeiro | 1963
Los Angeles | 1936 | 1492

0 *President Kennedy was shot in 1963.*
1 _____
2 _____
3 _____
4 _____
5 _____

have something done   SB page 59

5 ★★☆ Read about the hotel, then complete the letter.

Welcome to the
Ritz Carlton Hotel!

We have everything you need for the perfect weekend.

0 We park your car on arrival.
1 We take your bags to your room.
2 A top chef cooks all your meals.
3 Room service brings your meals to your room.
4 We deliver tickets to top shows to your room.
5 We wash and iron all your clothes.
6 A top stylist cuts your hair for free.

We had a wonderful weekend at the Ritz hotel.

0 *We had our car parked for us when we arrived.*
1 _____
2 _____
3 _____
4 _____
5 _____
6 _____

6 ★★★ **What did these people have done yesterday? Write sentences.**

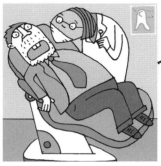
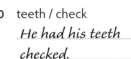

0   teeth / check

He had his teeth checked.

1   hair / dye

_____

2   pizza / deliver

_____

3   washing machine / fix

_____

Future and present perfect passive (review) `SB page 61`

7 ★☆☆ **Complete the text with the words in the list.**

haven't been painted | will be sold | will be shown
will be finished | has been made | will be put up
have been built | haven't been widened

It's only six months until the Olympic Games open here, but is the city ready? All of the stadiums
[1]_____ but many of them [2]_____
yet. The builders promise that they [3]_____
before the opening day. The city airport
[4]_____ bigger to allow more planes to land here but the roads from the airport into the city
[5]_____ and many people think the traffic will be a huge problem. Most of the tickets have been sold already and the organisers believe all of them
[6]_____ in the next few weeks. So if you're planning to come, make sure you get yours soon. Big screens [7]_____ around the city and many events [8]_____ live on them, so even if you can't get into the stadiums, you can enjoy the amazing Olympic atmosphere in this beautiful city.

8 ★★☆ **Complete the sentences with the present perfect passive form of the verbs in brackets.**

1   The windows are really dirty. They
_____ (not clean) for months.

2   Have you heard the news? The bank robbers
_____ (catch).

3   The test _____ (mark). You can find out your score online.

4   We've been waiting for an hour and our pizza still
_____ (not deliver).

5   Hey! Your bill _____ (not pay) yet.

9 ★★★ **Rewrite the sentences using the passive.**

1   They'll play the final on Thursday.

_____

2   They won't pay me until next month.

_____

3   A famous actor will open the new shopping centre.

_____

4   They've closed the hospital.

_____

5   The earthquake has destroyed the whole city.

_____

6   No one has seen them for days.

_____

GET IT RIGHT!
Future passive

Learners sometimes use the wrong tense where the future passive is required, or use the future passive where it is not required.

✓ The changes **will be introduced** next year.
✗ The changes ~~will introduce~~ next year.
✗ The changes ~~are introduced~~ next year.

Correct the errors in the sentences.

1   This money will use to develop the city.

_____

2   In the future the population will be increased.

_____

3   If the concert doesn't start soon, we are forced to leave.

_____

4   Please see the questionnaire which will be enclosed with this letter.

_____

5   The programme will show on Friday at 10 am.

_____

VOCABULARY

Make and do

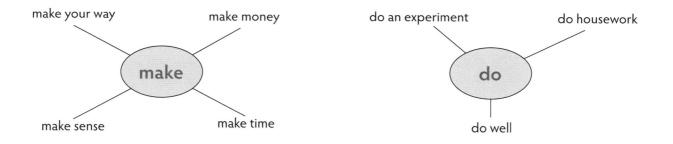

Key words in context

apparently	**Apparently** that trick is done with mirrors. I'm not sure exactly how though.
concerned	Tim's teacher is a bit **concerned** about him. She thinks he's not working as hard as he used to.
disbelief	There was a look of **disbelief** on her face – as if she'd seen a ghost.
fake	It's not a real Picasso. It's a **fake**.
float	The magician made the lady **float** up into the air.
illusion	The lady didn't really disappear. It was just a clever **illusion.**
onlooker	**Onlookers** watched in horror as the two men robbed the old lady in the middle of the street.
spectator	There were more than 30,000 **spectators** at the final.
support	One corner of the table is **supported** by a pile of books.

Extreme adjectives and modifiers
SB page 58

1 ★☆☆ **Find ten extreme adjectives in the wordsearch and write them next to the non-extreme adjectives.**

G	R	E	A	T	T	L	U	F	W	A
N	P	G	B	E	N	I	B	V	W	D
I	Y	A	Q	R	A	K	C	G	J	E
T	T	E	F	R	I	O	O	K	E	L
A	V	T	C	I	L	P	E	P	N	I
N	W	U	O	B	L	N	L	B	O	G
I	G	N	I	L	I	O	B	C	R	H
C	R	I	I	E	R	F	O	P	M	T
S	U	M	N	I	B	E	F	K	O	E
A	A	B	L	I	H	Y	T	F	U	D
F	A	N	T	A	S	T	I	C	S	D

interesting ¹ _____

happy ² _____

big ³ _____

good (x3) ⁴_____ ⁵_____ ⁶_____

bad (x2) ⁷_____ ⁸_____

hot ⁹ _____

small ¹⁰ _____

2 ★★☆ **Complete the sentences with extreme or ordinary adjectives.**

1 The play wasn't funny – it was absolutely h_____ .

2 Their new baby isn't s_____ – it's really tiny.

3 Our holiday wasn't just good – it was w_____ .

4 I wasn't s_____ – I was absolutely terrified.

5 Dad isn't sad – he's really m_____ .

6 It's not c_____ outside – it's absolutely freezing.

7 The new shopping centre isn't big – it's absolutely h_____ .

8 The rollercoaster ride wasn't e_____ – it was thrilling.

9 The book wasn't i_____ – it was fascinating.

10 They weren't just g_____ , they were amazing!

3 ★★☆ **Choose the correct word a or b. If both are possible choose c (both).**

1 We spent our holiday in Brazil and it was _____ boiling.

   a very   **b** absolutely   **c** both

2 Have you seen their house? It's _____ enormous!

   a very   **b** absolutely   **c** both

3 I liked the film. I thought it was _____ funny.

   a very   **b** absolutely   **c** both

4 Put a coat on. It's _____ cold outside.

   a very   **b** really   **c** both

5 I think the idea of time travel is _____ fascinating.

   a very   **b** absolutely   **c** both

6 She's an artist. Her paintings are _____ good.

   a very   **b** really   **c** both

make and *do*   **SB page 61**

4 ★☆☆ **Complete the sentences with *make* or *do*.**

1 It just doesn't _____ any sense to me.

2 There must be easier ways to _____ money.

3 Maybe it's time to _____ some housework.

4 Can you _____ your own way? I'm a bit busy at the moment.

5 I don't usually _____ this kind of experiment but I don't see what can go wrong.

6 Jack's been quite lonely since his best friend moved away. We should _____ time to see him this weekend.

5 ★★☆ **Match the sentences in Exercise 4 with the pictures.**

READING

1 REMEMBER AND CHECK Match the places and the events. Then check your answers in the article on page 57 of the Student's Book.

1 Central London ☐
2 The banks of the River Thames ☐
3 On the River Thames ☐
4 Bradford ☐
5 New Orleans ☐

a Crowds watch a man walk out onto the river.
b Dynamo's home town.
c Dynamo gets into a police boat.
d Dynamo falls in love with magic.
e Dynamo waves to crowds from a bus.

2 Read the article. What is the name of his performance in the picture? _____

HOW DOES HE DO IT?

When the American magician David Blaine started his professional career, people were soon talking about the originality of his shows. However, David had more ambitious plans and started a series of amazing public performances each designed to push his body further and further to its limits. Here are a few:

BURIED ALIVE

In April 1999, David performed his first major public stunt. For seven days he was buried underground in a tiny plastic box in New York. A large tank of water was placed on top of the box and the only way he could communicate was with a handheld electric buzzer. He ate nothing and drank just three tablespoons of water a day. Around 75,000 people visited the site to see David.

ABOVE THE BELOW

In September 2003, David took his show to Europe. For 44 days he lived in a transparent plastic box which was hung nine metres in the air on the banks of the River Thames in London. During this time he ate nothing and drank just four and a half litres of water a day. A webcam inside the box filmed the whole event live. The large crowds that came to watch were not always kind with objects such as eggs, bottles and golf balls being thrown at the box. When he came out of the box, David was taken straight to hospital because he was very weak from eating nothing.

DROWNED ALIVE

In May 2006, David climbed into a large globe filled with water, which was to be his home for the next week. All that connected him to the outside world were two tubes, one for air and the other to provide food. To finish the performance David planned to try and break the world record for holding one's breath under water. However, after seven minutes and 12 seconds he had to be pulled from the water as he was in trouble. He failed by one minute and 50 seconds.

REVOLUTION

In November 2006, David entered a large globe that was hung up near Times Square in New York. He spent the next 52 hours without food or water while it turned eight times a minute before freeing himself and jumping down to the ground. To celebrate his success he took 100 poor children to a local store where they were each given $500 to spend.

ELECTRIFIED

In October 2012, David spent 72 hours on top of a pillar while more than one million volts of electricity were sent in his direction. He wore a special suit to protect him and make sure that none of the electricity entered his body. He didn't sleep or eat for the whole time. The whole performance was filmed and shown live on Youtube.

3 Read the article again. Which event(s) …

1 lasted for more than five days?

_____

2 didn't end exactly as he had hoped it would?

_____

3 failed to impress some of the audience?

_____

4 saw him trapped in a ball?

_____

5 did he wear special clothing for?

_____

6 saw him not even eat or drink water?

4 Which of David's stunts would you be most scared to do? Write a short paragraph explaining why.

Pronunciation
The /ʒ/ phoneme
Go to page 119.

DEVELOPING WRITING

Describing a process

1 Read the text and match the words in the list with the pictures.

1	pulp	2	wood fibres	3	bark	4	log	5	branch	6	roll of paper

 **A**
 **B**
 **C**

 **D**
 **E**
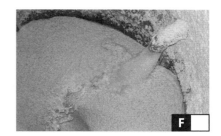 **F**

[1] We all know that paper comes from trees, but how exactly do you turn a solid piece of wood into the thin sheets of paper that we use every day?

[2] First of all the trees are cut down. This means, of course, that every year millions of new trees need to be planted to make sure there will be enough trees for future paper production.

[3] When the tree has been cut down the branches are taken off to make logs. The logs are loaded onto lorries and taken to the paper mill. At the paper mill, the logs are first put into a grinder machine where the outer layer of the tree, called the bark, is taken off. After that they are put into another machine where they are compressed tightly and broken into tiny pieces called fibre. Next, water is added to this fibre to make a thick soup-like liquid called pulp.

[4] This pulp is then sprayed into very thin sheets in a paper making machine. These sheets are passed under huge rollers which squeeze a lot of the water out. But the paper is still too wet so it is passed under heated rollers to dry it out completely. Finally the dry sheets of paper are rolled up ready to be taken from the paper mill.

2 In which paragraph is ...

1 the forest process described? ☐
2 the paper mill process described? ☐
3 the subject introduced? ☐
4 the final process described? ☐

3 Put the forest process in order. Then write the process in a short paragraph. Use *firstly*, *next*, *after that* and *finally*.

In the forest

☐ Branches taken off
☐ Logs taken to paper mill
☐ Trees cut down
☐ Logs loaded onto lorries

4 Choose one of the processes below (or one of your own) and write a short text of about 200 words to describe it.

- How dried pasta is made
- How glass is made
- How ice cream is made
- How politicians are elected

CHECKLIST

☐ Use words to describe a process
☐ Explain the process in order
☐ Explain how the process is finished

LISTENING

1 🔊 24 **Put the instructions for the card trick in order. Then listen and check.**

How to amaze your friends with a card trick.

1 'I will now find your card from these ones on the table.' ☐

2 'Put your card on top of the bottom part of the pack.' ☐

3 'Choose any card from the pack. Don't tell me what it is.' ☐

4 'Is this your card?' ☐

2 🔊 24 **Listen again. Complete the sentences from the listening with the missing words.**

1 _____, ask your friend to choose a card and look at it secretly.

2 _____ cut the pack of cards into two.

3 _____ _____, ask your friend to put the card on the top of the bottom part of the pack.

4 _____, put the pack back together and go through the cards.

3 🔊 25 **Listen and order the pictures.**

How to put on a transfer.

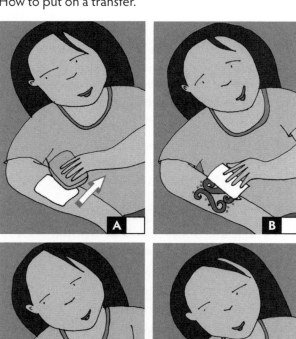

A ☐   B ☐   C ☐   D ☐

4 🔊 25 **Listen again and complete the instructions.**

1 _____, put the transfer paper on your arm, or wherever you want to put it.

2 _____ put a wet sponge (it shouldn't be too wet) on top and press hard.

3 _____ about a minute you can take the sponge away.

4 _____, slowly pull the paper away. It should leave the transfer on your skin.

DIALOGUE

1 **Put the dialogue in the correct order.**

☐	MAN	Three minutes. I'll remember that next time.
☐	MAN	For about five minutes.
☐	MAN	No, I didn't. I didn't know I had to.
☐	MAN	No, I didn't. I was far too hungry.
1	MAN	Oh dear. I've really made a mess of this egg. What did I do wrong?
☐	WOMAN	Finally, did you wait for a minute before you started to eat it?
☐	WOMAN	That's the first thing you should always do. How long did you cook it for?
☐	WOMAN	That's far too long. Three minutes is all you need.
☐	WOMAN	Did you wash the uncooked egg?

2 **Complete the conversation with the words in the list.**

Now | First | then | finally | After | online

MILLIE Hi, Mum. Are you having trouble with something?

MUM Yes, I want to post this photograph [1]_____ but I don't know how to do it.

MILLIE OK, let me help you. [2]_____, click here; where it says 'photo/video'.

MUM Ah, OK.

MILLIE [3]_____ that, click on 'upload photo'. Great! [4]_____ it's asking you which photo you want to upload.

MUM OK. I want this one here.

MILLIE OK, so just double-click on that. And [5]_____ write something about the photo if you want.

MUM All right.

MILLIE And [6]_____, click on 'post' and that's it! You've finished!

Reading and Use of English part 5

1 You are going to read another extract from *The Mind Map*. For questions 1–4, choose the answer (A, B, C or D) which you think fits best according to the text. Look back at the exam guide in Unit 5 on how to answer this question type.

The Mind Map by David Morrison

Eva was thinking hard. She looked past Lucho. He turned and saw that she was looking at a little yellow bird which had landed on the grass behind him.

'I've seen this bird a lot recently,' he said. 'Maybe it's trying to help me.'

Eva corrected him, 'Maybe it's trying to help us, Lucho.'

Lucho smiled.

'Come on,' he said. 'Let's follow it.'

Lucho pulled Eva up by the hand and they followed the little bird over the grass, towards the door to the school building. When they reached the door, Mr Parra, the history teacher, was walking out of the building.

'How is your mind map going, you two?' Mr Parra asked.

Lucho was not sure what to say. They couldn't tell Mr Parra that the mind map seemed to be alive.

'It's going well, sir,' said Eva, 'but we've got a question to ask you. Do you know what 'Ichua' means?'

Mr Parra smiled.

'Ichua is the name of the most important place in the world for the Kogi,' he explained. 'Their most important chiefs are buried there. The Kogi say it is a secret underground place full of gold, but historians don't believe that it's a real place. I see you have spent your time well in the library.'

It was Lucho's turn to ask a question. 'Mr Parra, do you know if there is a hotel in Santa Marta called the Hotel Continental?'

'Why?' Mr Parra was laughing. 'Are you planning a holiday?'

'No, sir,' answered Lucho, feeling a little stupid.

'Well, there was a hotel called the Hotel Continental in Santa Marta, near the port. But it closed a few years ago,' Mr Parra explained.

Eva watched the little yellow bird fly up to the roof of the library.

'Any more questions?' Mr Parra asked.

'Yes,' said Eva. 'Are birds important in Kogi stories?'

'Oh yes, Eva. There is a bird in every Kogi story. A bird brings a message to the jaguar or it helps the jaguar in its work. The jaguar, of course, is the most important animal for the Kogi and for many other tribes. The jaguar looks after the Kogi. Without the help of the jaguar, the Kogi believe, the sun would not rise, plants would not grow and rain would not fall.'

Mr Parra smiled.

'I must say I am very pleased that you have been working so well. Don't forget to put all the information on your mind map and bring it to class on Monday.'

Eva and Lucho watched Mr Parra as he walked away from the school building. Lucho's head was full of questions. Had he dreamed that the mind map had grown? Had he added new words in his sleep? But then, why had the message 'TAKE IT BACK' appeared on the computer screen and on Eva's mobile phone? What did the pendant want? Did he have to take it back to Ichua? But how could he? Mr Parra had said that Ichua probably wasn't a real place.

1 Eva corrects Lucho about the bird because …

A he doesn't know what kind of bird it is.

B she wants to let him know that she's decided to help him.

C he misunderstands how the bird is trying to help them.

D she thinks they should follow it.

2 Which of these statements is not true about Mr Parra?

A He teaches history at the school.

B He gave Lucho and Eva the mind map homework.

C He is happy that the children are taking their homework seriously.

D He was walking in the same direction as the children when they met him.

3 What do we learn about the Kogi from their stories?

A They are the only tribe for whom the jaguar is an important animal.

B They like birds.

C They put jaguars in all their stories.

D Nature is very important to them.

4 What does the final paragraph suggest about Lucho?

A He thinks he might be doing things in his sleep.

B He wanted to ask Mr Parra more questions.

C He's sure he's started to imagine things.

D He's really confused about the whole mind map mystery.

CONSOLIDATION

LISTENING

1 🔊 **26** Listen and (circle) A, B or C.

1 How long did the story for homework have to be?
   A 50,000 words
   B 5,000 words
   C 500 words

2 What did the story have to be about?
   A ghosts
   B crime
   C romance

3 If the teacher likes his story, the boy might …
   A help the girl to write one.
   B send it to a website.
   C publish it in the school magazine.

2 🔊 **26** **Listen again and answer the questions.**

1 Why does the boy enjoy homework that involves writing a story?

_____

2 How does he usually get an idea for a story?

_____

3 How long did he spend writing the story?

_____

4 Where did he get the idea for the story from?

_____

5 What does the girl want the boy to do?

_____

GRAMMAR

3 (Circle) the correct options.

1 There was an accident and a lot of people *hurt / were hurt*.

2 These books *are written / were written* a very long time ago.

3 The new school *will be opened / will open* by the mayor tomorrow.

4 I don't understand computers, so I always *repair my computer / have my computer repaired* when there's a problem.

5 In the last two years, they *have built / have been built* a lot of new buildings here.

6 I went to the hairdresser's and *cut my hair / had my hair cut*.

7 Thirty people *have taken / have been taken* to hospital.

8 Doctors *operate / are operated* on more than 30 people here every day.

4 Complete the sentences with *who, whose, where, that* or *which*.

1 That's the school _____ Dad taught.

2 Mr Newson, my maths teacher, is someone _____ I've learned a lot from.

3 I've forgotten _____ book this is.

4 Newquay, _____ is a small town in the south of England, is where my sister lives.

5 Careful, it's the dog _____ tried to bite me.

6 Look, that's the guy _____ was on the news last night.

VOCABULARY

5 Complete the words.

1 I thought the play was a _____ fantastic.

2 Some of the things were so funny – in fact, they were h_____ .

3 One actor said something that didn't make s_____ to me, but it didn't matter.

4 One actor was very young, but she did very well – she was b_____ , in fact.

5 She took the part of the evil v_____ in the play.

6 We were all very happy that we saw the play – in fact we were d_____ !

7 The theatre was very big – I've never seen such an e_____ theatre in my life!

8 It was a bit noisy so sometimes I couldn't hear the d_____ on stage very well.

6 Complete the conversation with the words in the list.

characters | crime | ending | hero | plot | setting | villain

STEVE   I read a good book last week. It was called *Detective Grange Investigates*.

EMILY   What's it about?

STEVE   Well, it's a ¹_____ novel. The ²_____ is London at the end of the 19th Century. And of course the ³_____ of the story is Detective Grange.

EMILY   And what's the ⁴_____?

STEVE   Well, it's about how Grange finds out who stole some money from a rich family's house. Grange meets all kinds of different people – there are some funny ⁵_____ and some horrible ones! The worst person is Dangerous Dan – he's the ⁶_____ of the story. At the end …

EMILY   No, no! Don't tell me the ⁷_____! I might read the book myself!

DIALOGUE

7 **Complete the conversation with the phrases in the list. There are two extra phrases.**

it isn't strange | let me finish | the strangest thing happened | what are the chances
you'll never believe | what's strange | that's the annoying thing | I don't understand

JAKE ¹_____ to me last weekend. I had a dream on Sunday about being lost in a completely empty city.

SUSIE ²_____ about that? People have dreams all the time – including about being lost.

JAKE I know. But the next day on TV there was a film where a woman was lost in an empty city, too – just like my dream. ³_____ of that happening?

SUSIE Well, not big, I suppose. But it's only a coincidence, isn't it?

JAKE No, ⁴_____ . There's more! You see, in the film, when the woman was lost, she started to hear a loud noise, like a wild animal or something. And ⁵_____ what happened next! A tiger suddenly appeared in front of her! Now, in my dream, I started to hear a strange noise too!

SUSIE And did a tiger appear in your dream?

JAKE Well, ⁶_____ . You see, just when the noise started, I woke up! So I don't know if there was a tiger in my dream or not. But my cat was lying on my bed!

READING

8 **Read the book review and answer the questions.**

1 What kind of stories was Paul Auster looking for?
   A real stories that weren't too long
   B the listeners' favourite stories
   C true stories about famous people

2 Why did he decide to put the stories in the book?
   A because he wanted to share them all with the public
   B to make some money
   C because he couldn't read them all out on the radio

3 What does the reviewer recommend?
   A to read the book from start to finish
   B to pick and choose stories from the book
   C to only read the sections you are most interested in

4 What is the reviewer's overall opinion of the book?
   A He liked it because the stories are so well written.
   B He liked it because some of the stories are very moving.
   C He liked another book of real-life stories more.

Review:
True Tales of American Life

In 1999, the writer Paul Auster was asked if he would contribute stories to America's National Public Radio. But Auster decided to ask listeners to send in their stories instead. He wanted true stories that seemed like fiction. They could be about anything at all, they just had to be true and short; the ones chosen would be read aloud on the radio.

To Auster's surprise, more than 4000 listeners sent in stories. It would have been impossible to read them all on the radio, so Auster took almost 200 of them and put them in a book – this book.

I liked some things about the collection, others not so much. Because the stories were written by ordinary people, they're not always well-written (I hate to think what the ones that weren't included were like!). And the categorisation into sections like *Families*, *Objects*, *Strangers*, or *Animals* means that if you read one story after the other, it can be a bit repetitive. But with any book of separate stories, you can just read one here and there whenever you feel like it, you don't have to read it straight through: and that's probably the best thing to do here, too.

What's great about these stories is their veracity – they're all true, no matter how unbelievable (and some of them really are incredible). One or two of the stories left me almost in tears, they were so painful.

So, overall it's worth getting and reading. If you're into real-life stories like these, I'd also recommend a collection called *The Moth* – more on this next time.

WRITING

9 Write a brief review of a story that you like – perhaps from a film, TV programme, book, or even a true story about you or a friend. Write 150–200 words.

7 ALL THE SAME?

GRAMMAR

make / let and *be allowed to* `SB page 68`

1 ★☆☆ **Write *make* or *let* in each space.**

Here is what life is like at the summer camp. Some things are great – others, not so much!

1 They _____ us watch TV every evening until 10.30.

2 They _____ us clean our shoes every day.

3 They _____ us tidy the things in our room at the end of every day.

4 They _____ us check emails twice a day.

5 They _____ us listen to our own music in our rooms.

6 They _____ us take a cold shower every day.

7 They _____ us sleep late on Saturdays and Sundays.

8 They _____ us eat vegetables with every meal.

2 ★★☆ **Rewrite the sentences using *make / doesn't make / lets / doesn't let*.**

0 MUM You have to wash up after dinner.
Mum makes me wash up after dinner.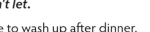

1 DAD You can stay out later on Saturdays.
_____

2 MUM You can't play loud music in the house.
_____

3 MUM You don't have to tidy your room.
_____

4 MUM You don't have to get up early on Sundays.
_____

5 DAD You can't drive my car.
_____

6 DAD You have to put the rubbish out.
_____

7 DAD You can bring friends round at the weekend.
_____

3 ★★★ **Look at the signs. Rewrite them using *You're (not) allowed to*.**

0 *You're not allowed to cycle in the park.*

1 _____
_____

2 _____
_____

3 _____
_____

4 _____
_____

5 _____
_____

6 _____
_____

7 _____
_____

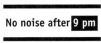

No noise after 9 pm

Feel free to use our computers

No entry to under 16s

Library borrowing
four books at a time

4 ★★★ **Complete the sentences so that they are true for you.**

1 I'm not allowed to _____

2 My friends never let me _____

3 At school, we're allowed to _____

4 Our teacher doesn't let us _____

5 I don't like it when someone makes me _____

6 It isn't fair to make someone _____

5 ★★★ Use the prompts to form questions using *make / let / be allowed to*.

0 parents / you / help with the housework?

Do your parents make you help with
the housework?

1 teachers / you / do homework every night?

_____

2 you / send text messages in class?

_____

3 school / you / go into any room you want?

_____

4 parents / you / sleep as long as you like?

_____

5 you / eat anything you want at home?

_____

6 parents / you / stay out after midnight?

_____

6 ★★★ Write your answers to the questions in Exercise 5.

0 _____

1 _____

2 _____

3 _____

4 _____

5 _____

6 _____

be / get used to SB page 69

7 ★☆☆ Match the sentence halves.

1 When we went to Los Angeles, it took us time ☐

2 She was a bit nervous because ☐

3 It isn't always easy ☐

4 At first my mum didn't like working from home, ☐

5 My brother is learning Arabic and he has to ☐

6 When my sister joined the police, she ☐

7 He didn't like the cat at first because ☐

8 Can I have a knife and fork please? ☐

a she wasn't used to travelling alone.

b get used to writing from right to left.

c had to get used to wearing a uniform.

d to get used to the American accent.

e he was used to having dogs at home.

f I'm not used to using chopsticks.

g but then she got used to it.

h to get used to life in a different country.

8 ★★☆ For each sentence, use *be used to* or *get used to* and a verb from the list in the correct form.

live | eat | read | go | (not) hug

1 Before I went to China, I _____ with a knife and fork, but then I _____ with chopsticks.

2 Back home, when I had a job, I _____ to work by train, so I had to _____ to work by bus in China.

3 I also had to _____ people very much – it wasn't easy because in my country, we _____ our family and friends a lot!

4 And of course in my language, I _____ things in the Roman alphabet, but when I started to learn Chinese, I had to _____ special characters.

5 So now I _____ in China, but I won't live here forever – in two years I'll go back home, I think.

GET IT RIGHT!

be used to vs. *get used to*

Learners have difficulty in telling the difference between *be used to something* and *get used to something*.

We use *be used to* to say that we are familiar with something now.

✓ *My friends in Spain find it strange that we eat dinner at 6 pm, but it's normal for us, we're used to it.*

✗ *My friends in Spain find it strange that we eat dinner at 6 pm, but it's normal for us, we ~~get used to it~~.*

We use *get used to* to talk about the process of becoming familiar with something over time.

✓ *When I first came to the UK, I found it strange to eat dinner at 6 pm but after a while I got used to it.*

✗ *When I first came to the UK, I found it strange to eat dinner at 6 pm, but after a while I ~~am used to it~~.*

Ⓒircle the correct word, *be* or *get*.

1 Swimming practice was hard at first, but I *am / got* used to it eventually.

2 It's easy to get up at 8 am, now that I'*m / got* used to it.

3 I finally *am / got* used to the rain in Manchester after a few months.

4 He didn't like his new school, but after a few weeks he *is / got* used to it.

5 Understanding her English teacher was hard for a while but she *is / got* used to her now.

6 *Are you / Did you get* used to the food here now?

VOCABULARY

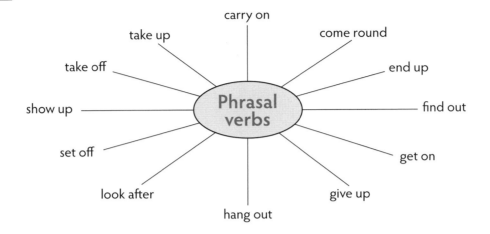

carry on · take up · come round · take off · end up · show up · find out · set off · get on · look after · give up · hang out

Phrasal verbs

Personality

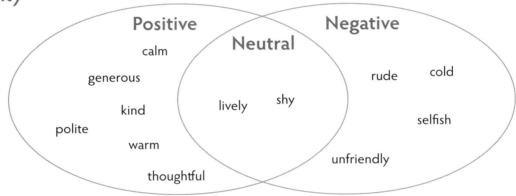

Positive · Neutral · Negative

calm · generous · kind · polite · warm · thoughtful

lively · shy

rude · cold · selfish · unfriendly

Phrases with *all*

after all
all day
all the same
all (we're) saying (is)
for all I know
once and for all

Key words in context

bend	The road isn't straight – after 100 metres, it **bends** to the right.
coal miner	He was a **coal miner** for forty years and he had a lot of health problems.
convince	She tried to **convince** me that her favourite band is better than The Beatles!
nerd	She spends all her time thinking about computers – she's a real IT **nerd.**
prisoner	It's a big prison – there are more than a thousand **prisoners** there.
professional	She's a good singer, but perhaps not good enough to turn **professional**.
scholarship	I got a **scholarship** to this school, so my parents don't have to pay.
stereotype	I didn't think the people in the film were realistic. I thought they were **stereotypes**.

Phrasal verbs (1) `SB page 68`

1 ★☆☆ **Match the verbs and their definitions.**

1	look after	**a**	stop doing something (often a bad habit)
2	take up	**b**	discover
3	show up	**c**	start a journey
4	give up	**d**	take care of, or be in charge of
5	carry on	**e**	begin (a hobby or new subject)
6	find out	**f**	like a person and be friends with them
7	get on	**g**	continue
8	set off	**h**	arrive at a place (often late or unexpectedly)

2 ★★☆ **Use the phrasal verbs in Exercise 1 in the correct form to complete the sentences.**

1 They were so late! We agreed to meet at 7.30 but they only _____ at 8.15!

2 We started playing at three in the afternoon, and we _____ until it got dark.

3 Sam was so happy when he _____ that he'd won the competition.

4 They're always arguing – they don't _____ at all.

5 My grandfather's ill so my mum is _____ him.

6 We _____ at eight in the morning and by midday, we were there!

7 The exam was too hard! After twenty minutes I _____ and left the room.

8 My dad was getting bored at home, so he _____ bird watching and now he's out all the time.

Personality `SB page 71`

3 ★☆☆ **Use the clues to complete the puzzle.**

1 It was very ____ of you to offer to help.

2 I didn't like him – he was very ___ .

3 I like her – she's a very ___ person.

4 It's 'me, me, me' all the time – she's so ___ .

5 I like her smile – it's so ___ and welcoming.

6 He always says things nicely – he's very ___ .

7 Please don't laugh at me – it's very ___ .

8 She won't come and talk to you – she's too ___ .

```
1 [ ][ ][ ][G][ ][ ][ ][ ]
2 [ ][ ][ ][E][ ][ ][ ]
       3 [ ][N][ ]
      4 [ ][ ][E][ ][ ][ ]
     5 [ ][ ][R][ ][ ]
       6 [ ][O][ ][ ][ ]
      7 [ ][U][ ]
        8 [ ][S][ ][ ]
```

4 ★★☆ **Use personality adjectives to complete the sentences about each person. Use the first letter of the person's name to help you.**

1 Linda is _____   2 Steve is _____

I'll pay!

3 Chris is _____   4 Gina is _____

WordWise `SB page 73`
Phrases with *all*

5 ★★☆ **Use an expression with *all* to complete each sentence.**

1 Of course I'll help you.
_____ , you're my friend!

2 I've been working on this problem _____ and I still haven't finished!

3 **A** Who's that guy over there?

B I've got no idea. He could be anyone, _____ .

4 You've asked me that question five times! _____ , I don't know – OK?

5 Look, I know it's your favourite film. _____ is that I didn't like it very much. All right?

6 Well, we can go to the cinema or to the park. It's _____ to me.

READING

1 REMEMBER AND CHECK **Answer the questions by writing *Billy* or *Jess*. Then check your answers in the article on page 67 of the Student's Book.**

Who …

1 scores a winning goal? _____

2 has a father who is a coal miner? _____

3 goes to study in California? _____

4 goes to study in London? _____

5 becomes a top professional? _____

6 sends a photo home? _____

7 has to do an entrance test? _____

8 is part of an Indian family? _____

9 has a sister who's getting married? _____

10 has a teacher called Georgia? _____

11 has a trainer called Joe? _____

12 gets help from people in
the town? _____

2 Read the quotations on the blog page. Choose the title you think best fits the page.

- [ ] A Are we all the same?
- [ ] B People are people
- [ ] C Everyone is different

3 Put these phrases into the correct places in the blog.

A the same air

B all the same

C laugh at you

D I treat my friends

E the same way

F your eyes

G their circumstances

4 Which quotations talk …

1 about people being the same?

_____

2 about people being different?

_____

SHARE >

Dan's Daily Discussions

I asked people to say something about people and stereotypes. This is what you sent. I call this collection: _____

1. At the end of the day, we're human beings and that's that. You can challenge stereotypes by just being who you are. – *Stephanie Cox*

2. Wasn't it Ernest Hemingway who said that every man's life ends ☐? It's just how we live and how we die that distinguish us from each other.
– *Mike Gillespie*

3. I think it's beautiful that everyone is different. If we were ☐, it would be boring. – *Jenny Price*

4. My grandma always said that people are people. She was rich but she treated everyone the same way. And that's why I treat our dustman the same way ☐. Because people are people. – *Sarah White*

5. When it's dark, we're all the same. There are nice people and not nice people, it doesn't matter what colour they are. Don't let ☐ fool you. – *Agata Morris*

6. John Kennedy said that we share lots of things. We all live on Planet Earth and we all breathe ☐. We think about our children's future. And we'll all die one day. – *Paul Gibson*

7. I think people are all the same, really. We're born in different places and in different cultures. People are all the same, though ☐ differ in hundreds of ways.
– *George Henderson*

8. Someone once said that there are two kinds of people: those who divide the world into two kinds of people, and those who don't. – *Janie Smith*

9. A friend of mine who had white hair when she was twenty said: You laugh at me because I'm different. I ☐ because you're all the same. – *Mandy Atkins*

DEVELOPING WRITING

A blog about a different country

1   Read the blog. Which of the things in the photos does Frances mention?

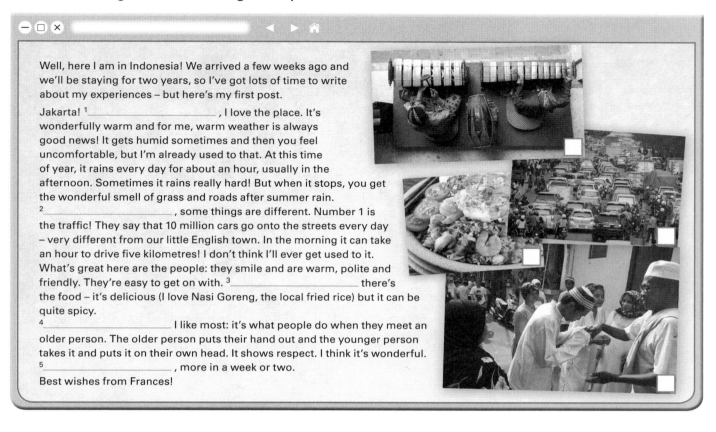

Well, here I am in Indonesia! We arrived a few weeks ago and we'll be staying for two years, so I've got lots of time to write about my experiences – but here's my first post.

Jakarta! ¹_____ , I love the place. It's wonderfully warm and for me, warm weather is always good news! It gets humid sometimes and then you feel uncomfortable, but I'm already used to that. At this time of year, it rains every day for about an hour, usually in the afternoon. Sometimes it rains really hard! But when it stops, you get the wonderful smell of grass and roads after summer rain.

²_____ , some things are different. Number 1 is the traffic! They say that 10 million cars go onto the streets every day – very different from our little English town. In the morning it can take an hour to drive five kilometres! I don't think I'll ever get used to it. What's great here are the people: they smile and are warm, polite and friendly. They're easy to get on with. ³_____ there's the food – it's delicious (I love Nasi Goreng, the local fried rice) but it can be quite spicy.

⁴_____ I like most: it's what people do when they meet an older person. The older person puts their hand out and the younger person takes it and puts it on their own head. It shows respect. I think it's wonderful.

⁵_____ , more in a week or two.

Best wishes from Frances!

2   Read the blog again and answer the questions.

1   How long is Frances going to live in Jakarta?

_____

2   What thing(s) does Frances find very different in Jakarta?

_____

3   Which thing(s) does she dislike? How do you know?

_____

4   What is her favourite thing about Indonesia?

_____

3   Complete the blog with the phrases in the list.

Anyway | Here's what | Then | So far | Of course

4   Imagine you have gone to live in another country. How is it different to your home country? Make a list of things you have to get used to in this new country, or are already used to. Use the ideas in the blog to help you.

1   _____

2   _____

3   _____

4   _____

INDONESIA

Jakarta

Island of Java

5   Now write a blog post about your new country using the notes you made in Exercise 4. Write about 250 words.

CHECKLIST ✔

☐   Write where you are.

☐   Write when you arrived.

☐   Write what things you like / dislike about the new country.

☐   Write what things you have got used to.

☐   Write what things you haven't got used to yet.

LISTENING

1 🔊 **27** Listen to two conversations. Answer the questions.

CONVERSATION 1

1 What are Sean's plans for the weekend?

_____

2 Where does Nadia invite him on Saturday night?

_____

3 Why doesn't he want to go at first?

_____

4 When should Sean phone Nadia?

_____

CONVERSATION 2

5 Where are Graham and his friends going on Sunday?

_____

6 Who can Sarah bring along with her?

_____

7 What time are they going to meet on Sunday?

_____

8 What does Sarah think about the meeting time?

_____

2 🔊 **27** Listen again. Complete these parts of the conversations.

1

NADIA	Well listen, some of us are going to the cinema on Saturday. Why ¹_____?
SEAN	The cinema? Well, I'm not a big fan.
NADIA	OK, no problem. See you Monday then.
SEAN	No, wait, just a minute. ²_____ come. What time on Saturday?
NADIA	I'm not sure yet. ³_____ me a call this evening?

2

SARAH	Wow – that sounds like a great idea.
GRAHAM	OK then. ⁴_____ along?
SARAH	That would be great – ⁵_____ . Thanks, Graham.
GRAHAM	No problem. ⁶_____ some friends along with you?
SARAH	OK, I'll call some people.

Pronunciation

Intonation – inviting, accepting and refusing invitations
Go to page 120. 🔊

DIALOGUE

1 Put the conversations in the correct order.

CONVERSATION 1

☐ A Well, how about coming with me to that new club in town?

[1] A Are you busy on Friday?

☐ A OK let's meet there at seven.

☐ B Fine. I'll see you there.

☐ B That would be great. I'd love to!

☐ B No, I'm not. Why?

CONVERSATION 2

☐ C Why don't you bring someone along?

[1] C Do you fancy going to a party tonight?

☐ C A friend of mine, Jake. It's his birthday.

☐ D No, that's OK. I'd rather just go with you.

☐ D Whose party is it?

☐ D OK, why not? I like parties.

PHRASES FOR FLUENCY   SB page 73

1 Put the words in order to make expressions.

0 point / good   *Good point*

1 it / mention / don't   _____

2 it / in / pack   _____

3 it / one / in / got   _____

4 me / don't / wrong / get   _____

5 this / with / I'm / one / you / on   _____

2 Use the phrases from Exercise 1 to complete the conversations.

1 A It's great that you're helping me. Thanks so much.

  B Oh, _____ . It's a pleasure.

2 A Come on, let's go out for a walk.

  B But the match is on TV in fifteen minutes.

  A Hmmm, _____ . Maybe we'll leave the walk until later.

3 A No, sorry – this music's really awful!

  B _____ , Terry. Let's listen to something else.

4 A So you didn't like the present I gave you?

  B Oh, no. _____ , I liked it. It's just that red isn't my favourite colour.

5 A Mum, Angie won't give me my football back. Please tell her to.

  B Oh, Bobby, _____ , please! I've got a really bad headache.

6 A So, why can't you come out tonight? Homework?

  B _____ . French, English and History!

Reading and Use of English part 3

1 For questions 1–10, read the text below. Use the word given in capitals at the end of some of the lines to form a word that fits in the gap in the same line. There is an example at the beginning (0).

A Trip of a Lifetime!

I'm not usually a very **(0)** _adventurous_ kind of person. I don't like having too much **ADVENTURE**

(1) _____ in my life, but the trip that I took on the river at the Iguaçu Falls between Brazil and **EXCITE**

Argentina was just fantastic and totally **(2)** _____ ! **FORGET**

We stayed in a small hotel in the town centre and the next day we got on a **(3)** _____ bus to **CROWD**

go to the Iguaçu Park, where the waterfalls are. We got off the bus near a very **(4)** _____ hotel **LUXURY**

– the only hotel in the park – and then walked down the path. You can go close to the waterfalls, and

you get very wet from the spray. The day we went, it was a bit **(5)** _____ but we took some **CLOUD**

great photographs anyway. The scenery is **(6)** _____ . **SPECTACLE**

Then we decided to go on a river trip to the falls. You get into an **(7)** _____ boat and ride up **INFLATE**

the river to the base of the waterfalls. The noise is **(8)** _____ loud! But you have to be a bit **INCREDIBLE**

careful because the water is rough and so it is a little bit **(9)** _____ to be there. **DANGER**

Back at our hotel, we had an hour of **(10)** _____ before dinner, and we talked about all the **RELAX**

fantastic things we had seen.

Exam guide: word formation

This is a test of your ability to form words in English. You have to read a text in which there are 10 empty spaces, and in each space you have to write the correct form of the key word in capital letters at the end of the line.

- You will usually need to change the grammatical form of the word – for example, change a verb to a noun, or a noun to an adjective, and so on. So, make sure you think about grammar.
- Some of the gaps will be easier than others – go through the text and do the ones you find easy first. Then go back and think about the harder ones.
- Remember, you might need to make a word negative (look at gap number 2 in task 1 above, for example).

2 For questions 1–10, read the text below. Use the word given in capitals at the end of some of the lines to form a word that fits in the gap in the same line. There is an example at the beginning (0).

The Sea View Bed and Breakfast – a review

We stayed here last month for three nights and had an **(0)** _enjoyable_ stay overall. **ENJOY**

We really liked the location – it's in the town centre, so restaurants and shops are very **(1)** _____ . **ACCESS**

And the scenery is quite nice too – there are very **(2)** _____ views over to the hills on the **ATTRACT**

other side. Breakfast is absolutely delicious, with an excellent **(3)** _____ of fruit. I love a cooked **SELECT**

breakfast too and the one here was **(4)** _____ good! Also, the staff could not have been more **BELIEVE**

attentive and **(5)** _____ . **FRIEND**

The bedroom was large and **(6)** _____ , and the bathroom was too. So, what was the problem? **SPACE**

We had three almost **(7)** _____ nights. The bed was the hardest and most **SLEEP**

(8) _____ bed I have ever tried to sleep in! And there was a street outside the bedroom which **COMFORT**

had almost **(9)** _____ noise throughout the night . **CONTINUE**

So it's **(10)** _____ that we would go back. It's a shame because the Sea View has so many good **DOUBT**

things going for it.

8 IT'S A CRIME

GRAMMAR
Reported speech (review) SB page 76

1 ★★☆ **Report what the mugger said to a friend. Complete the sentences using reported speech.**

0 'I mugged a girl yesterday.'

He said *he had mugged a girl the day* before.

1 'I stole her laptop.'

He said _____ her laptop.

2 'I felt really terrible about stealing it.'

He said _____ really terrible about stealing it.

3 'I am going to say sorry to her.'

He said _____ sorry to her.

4 'I will never mug anyone again.'

He said _____ anyone again.

2 ★★☆ **Rewrite these sentences using reported speech.**

1 'I'm really upset,' said Mrs Jones after the burglary.

_____

2 'The burglar went into the house through the bathroom window,' the man told the police.

_____

3 'This is the first time I've been caught shoplifting,' the woman told the manager of the shop.

_____

4 'I was waiting on the underground platform when it happened,' said the man.

_____

5 'Pickpockets in London can make £4000 a week by stealing wallets, smartphones and laptops,' a policeman told us.

_____

6 'I will think about putting cameras up in the shop,' the shopkeeper said after the robbery.

_____

7 'My son is going to report the mugging to the police,' said Mrs Roberts.

_____

3 ★★☆ **Rewrite what the people said in direct speech.**

0 The residents asked the police if they had arrested the mugger yet.

'Have you arrested the mugger yet?'

1 The security guard told the police that he had seen the shoplifter run across the car park.

_____

2 The shoplifter told the manager that he had never been in trouble with the police before.

_____

3 The man told the police that nobody was living in the house next door.

_____

4 The lawyer told the man that he would probably be sentenced to three years in prison.

_____

5 The woman said that she was going to report the theft to the police.

_____

Reported questions, requests and imperatives SB page 77

4 ★☆☆ (Circle) **the correct form of the verbs.**

1 'Sit down.'

The police officer told me *sit down / to sit down*.

2 'Write your statement on the form.'

He told me *write / to write* my statement on the form.

3 'Don't worry.'

He told me *not to worry / don't worry*.

4 'Did you see the burglar?'

He asked me if I *had seen / saw* the burglar.

5 'Do you live in this block of flats?'

He asked me whether I *lived / had lived* in this block of flats.

6 'Are you going to interview anyone else?'

I asked him if he *had interviewed / was going to interview* anyone else.

5 ★★☆ Complete the sentences.

1 'Write down your name and address.'

   He asked me _____

2 'Stand up.'

   She told us _____

3 'Do you know the victim?'

   He asked us _____

4 'Describe the mugger.'

   He asked me _____

5 'Fill in the form.'

   She told him _____

6 'Have you been burgled before?'

   He asked her _____

6 ★★☆ Match the sentences. Then complete the sentences.

1 'No I won't tell you where we've hidden the phones,' said the boy. ☐

2 'Where did you hide the phones?' asked the policeman. ☐

3 'No, I was in the car when they hid the phones,' said the boy. ☐

4 'Come to the police station and make a statement,' said the policeman. ☐

5 'You must tell me who the other two boys are,' said the policeman. ☐

6 'All right. I'll come to the station with you,' said the boy. ☐

7 'Can I phone my mum?' asked the boy. ☐

8 'Do you have a phone?' asked the policeman. ☐

a The boy asked if

   _____

b The policeman told the boy

   _____

c The policeman demanded to know

   _____

d The boy refused to tell the police

   _____

e The policeman asked the boy where

   _____

f The policeman asked the boy if

   _____

g The boy explained that

   _____

h The boy agreed

7 ★★★ Read the script for a play and report the dialogue.

> *James is waiting at a bus stop when two guys walk up to him.*
>
> **MUGGER** Do you want to survive tonight?
>
> **JAMES** I don't understand what you mean.
>
> **MUGGER** The night can have a good ending or a bad ending. It's up to you.
>
> **JAMES** Please tell me what you mean by that. Are you a mugger? I've only got £20.
>
> **MUGGER** That's fine.
>
> *[James gives him the money. The mugger moves closer. James is scared.]*
>
> **JAMES** Are you going to hurt me?
>
> **MUGGER** Thanks, mate.
>
> *[hugs the boy and walks off]*
> *James was surprised – he couldn't believe that the mugger had hugged him!*
>
> He asked me [1] _____
> I told him I [2] _____
> He said that the night [3] _____
> I asked him [4] _____
> I wanted to know [5] _____
> I told him that [6] _____
> He said that [7] _____
> I asked him [8] _____

GET IT RIGHT! ◉

Reported questions

In reported questions we don't use question word order, but statement word order.

✓ I'll ask where **I can** find the station.

✗ I'll ask where ~~can I~~ find the station.

We don't need the auxiliary *do*.

✓ They asked when **it started**.

✗ They asked when ~~did it start~~.

If it is a yes / no question, we need to include *if*.

✓ I'll ask **if** he has arrived yet.

✗ I'll ask ~~he~~ has arrived yet.

Correct the sentences.

1 He asked how much did I pay for the phone.

   _____

2 Everyone asked when did the article have to be finished.

   _____

3 I asked my mum I could go out.

   _____

4 I asked my mum which school will I go to when we move house.

   _____

VOCABULARY

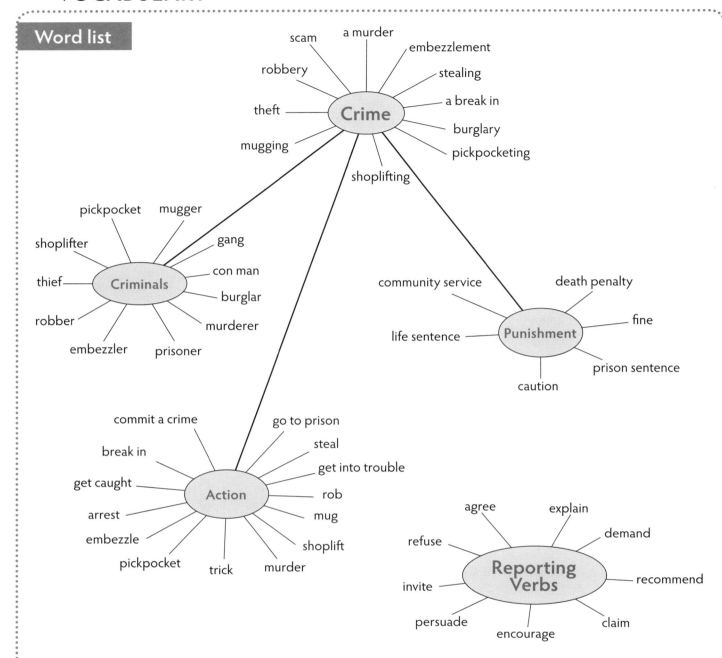

Key words in context

apology	I'm so sorry. Please accept my **apology**.
auction	The painting was sold at an **auction** recently.
bargain	It wasn't expensive, it was a real **bargain**.
deter	They are using cameras to **deter** pickpockets.
in common	James and Tony are brothers but they don't have much **in common**.
ironically	He's been living in Spain for ten years, but **ironically**, he speaks very little Spanish.
justice	The police are trying everything they can to bring the murderer to **justice**.
mortgage	They had to get a big **mortgage** in order to buy their house.
reporter	**Reporters** tried to interview the man for the local newspaper.
resident	The **residents** were shocked when they heard about the crime.
think twice	You should always **think twice** before you say something.
witness	A **witness** saw the robber go into the house.

Crime SB page 76

1 ★☆☆ **Who committed the crime? Complete the sentences with a criminal in the list.**

pickpocket | shoplifter | con man | thief | burglar | murderer

1 He was a famous _____ . Everyone fell for his scams.

2 The _____ left a knife next to his victim's dead body.

3 The _____ stole small amounts of money from people's purses while they were away from their desks.

4 She was travelling on the tube when she realised a _____ had taken her purse from her bag.

5 The _____ put 10 bracelets on her arm and then she walked out of the shop.

6 The woman heard the _____ breaking into her house and she called the police.

2 ★★☆ **These people all committed a crime. What did they do? Write a sentence for each.**

1 The mugger _____

2 The burglar _____

3 The con man _____

4 The pickpocket _____

5 The murderer _____

6 The shoplifter _____

3 ★★☆ **Read the clues and complete the puzzle with the punishments.**

1 the legal punishment of death for a crime

2 a warning given by a police officer to someone who has broken the law

3 work done without payment to help other people that criminals are sometimes ordered to do

4 an amount of money that has to be paid for breaking a rule or law

5 a person in prison for committing a crime

6 the punishment of being put in prison for a very long time, or, sometimes, until death

7 a punishment that means a person will have to spend time in a special building for criminals

8 to do something wrong and be found out

```
1 |   |   |   |   | ■ | P |   |   |   |   |   |
        2 |   | U |   |
3 |   |   |   |   | N |   |   | ■ |   |   |   |   |   |
              4 |   | I |   |
        5 |   |   |   | S |   |   |   |
                | H |
                | M |
6 |   |   |   | ■ | E |   |   |   |   |   |
    7 |   |   |   | N | ■ |   |   |   |   |   |   |
        8 |   | T | ■ |   |   |   | ■ |   |   |   |   |   |
```

Reporting verbs SB page 79

4 ★★☆ ⟨Circle⟩ **the correct reporting verb.**

1 'I won't go to the police station.'

The boy *refused* / *demanded* to go to the police station.

2 'I was in the garden when it happened.'

The woman *demanded* / *explained* that she had been in the garden when it happened.

3 'Yes, you're right. It's my fault.'

The man *agreed* / *told* that it was his fault.

4 'You have to tell me what happened.'

The policeman *demanded* / *claimed* to know what had happened.

5 'I was with my wife in a restaurant at 9 pm last night.'

The man *claimed* / *agreed* that he had been with his wife in a restaurant at 9 pm that night.

6 'Empty your pockets for me, please.'

The policeman *explained* / *told* him to empty his pockets.

7 'We're going to the museum. Would you like to come with us?'

They *persuaded* / *invited* me to go to the museum with them.

8 'If you like pizza, then Pizza Shed on the High Street is the place to go.'

She *recommended* / *invited* having pizza at Pizza Shed.

9 'I know the guitar can be difficult, but I think you should try to learn it.'

He *invited* / *encouraged* me to learn the guitar.

10 'OK, OK, I'll go to the concert with you.'

I *persuaded* / *agreed* her to go to the concert with me.

READING

1 **REMEMBER AND CHECK** Answer the questions. Then check your answers in the news story on page 75 of the Student's Book.

1 How did Margaret Atkins feel when she realised the bike had gone? _____

2 What did Margaret Atkins do instead of going to the police? _____

3 Why didn't she want to report the incident to the police? _____

4 What was Frank Caron the victim of? _____

5 Where had they seen the games console? _____

6 What did Mr Caron find inside the box when it arrived? _____

2 Read the text. What crime has the girl committed?

_____

CAUGHT

It all started when I was at university. I don't make friends easily and I was unhappy being away from home. I was also finding my courses at university very difficult. I went to see the doctor and he said I was depressed and suggested that I saw a therapist. The therapist told me that one way to feel better would be to 'pamper' myself – to do something good for myself. I liked the idea, but I was a student and I didn't have any money. Other than buying a big bar of chocolate occasionally, there was no way that I could afford to go shopping and treat myself.

It was then that I started to shoplift. I didn't realise how easy it was. By the end of university I knew all the places in the shops where no one would see me taking things. I was completely addicted to shoplifting. I could have anything I wanted and not pay any money at all. It felt fantastic.

One day, I decided to go into town and 'treat' myself. In one of the stores, a security guard saw me slip some things into my bag. Finally, I'd been caught shoplifting. The security guard took me to a room. I didn't make a fuss. I just went with him. He called the store manager, and they made me empty out all my bags. They wanted to see the receipts for everything. I only had receipts for two things. I'd taken stuff from six shops. When it was all out on the table, I looked at it all and I felt terrible. Standing there with the security guards and the store manager made me finally see myself as a thief.

I started crying and I apologised for stealing. I said that I would pay anything they wanted. They called the police because the stuff was worth a lot of money. Then they took down my name, address and date of birth.

The police made me take all the stuff I'd stolen back to the stores. They made me apologise to all the store managers. I've been banned from going to any of those stores again. I don't know what to do. I don't want my parents to find out that I'm a shoplifter. They'll be so disappointed in me. What's going to happen?

3 **Answer the questions.**

1 What reasons does she give for being unhappy?

_____

2 When did the girl start shoplifting?

_____

3 What did the therapist suggest she do?

_____

4 Why did she become addicted to shoplifting?

_____

5 Why did the store manager want to see the receipts?

_____

6 What did the police make her do?

_____

4 **What do you think should happen? Write a short reply to the girl.**

What punishment will she get? Should she tell her parents?

5 **Now read the end of her story and answer the questions.**

> I told my mum. She didn't get angry with me. She was very understanding. I've made an appointment with my therapist. The police told me that the stores have decided not to take me to court. I'll just pay a fine.

1 Do you think her mum's response was a good response? Why (not)?

_____

2 Do you think she deserves a heavier punishment? Why (not)?

_____

DEVELOPING WRITING

An essay about crime

1   **Read the essay quickly. What is it about?**

_____

2   **Read the essay again and label the headings below with the paragraphs A–E.**

Argument for ☐   The conclusion ☐   The writer's opinion ☐   Argument against ☐
Introduction summarising the debate ☐

Poverty is the Cause of Crime

A   Crime is a serious problem in every country around the world. Some people think that the main cause of crime is poverty. Other people have argued that poverty does not have a direct link to crime.

B   ¹_____ , there are many reasons why people commit crimes, and poverty is one of them. For example, a teenager has no money but wants the same trainers as his or her classmate so goes out and shoplifts them.

C   ²_____ , it's not just poor people who commit crimes. Wealthy people with good jobs and loving families also commit crimes. However, they probably commit their crimes for other reasons. ³_____ , they may be risk takers. ⁴_____ , children from a poor family with a very loving mother and father will probably not commit a crime. They have love and security and they're happy.

D   ⁵_____ , the main reason for teenagers and young people committing crimes is the lack of support from their family and people around them. They feel unloved and they have no good role models.

E   ⁶_____ , poverty is a cause of crime, but it is not the only cause. Governments need to improve living standards for all their citizens, and we all need to try and help children and teenagers who have no support from others.

3   **Complete the essay with the phrases in the list.**

To conclude | However | Firstly | For example | In my opinion | On the other hand

4   **Write an essay with the title 'Heavier Punishments Will Reduce Crime'.**

Planning your essay

- Think about the advantages and disadvantages of stronger criminal sentences.
- Add two advantages and two disadvantages to the columns.

Advantages	Disadvantages
It will deter criminals from committing another crime.	Mixing with other criminals in prison will do more harm than good.

Now you have your argument _for_ and _against_ heavier punishment. You also need:

- An introduction
- Your opinion
- A conclusion

Look again at the phrases in Exercise 3 above to help with your writing.

Write about 250 words.

CHECKLIST ✔

☐ Introduction   ☐ My thoughts
☐ Arguments for   ☐ Conclusion
☐ Arguments against   ☐ Connecting phrases

LISTENING

1 🔊 **30** **Listen to the dialogue. Mark the sentences T (true) or F (false).**

1 A parcel came through the letterbox the other day for Jane. ☐

2 The sender had paid too little for the postage. ☐

3 They wanted Jane to pay an extra £460. ☐

4 Jane never received the letter. ☐

5 Jane's friend doesn't think it was a large amount of money. ☐

6 The police told her that hundreds of people had been tricked by the scam. ☐

2 🔊 **30** **Listen again. Complete these parts of the conversation.**

1

A You'll never guess what I've done.

B Uh oh, Jane _____ !

A I've been really stupid.

2

A Yes, I paid it online.

B _____ ?

A Yes, really. I was curious about the letter. I wondered who it was from.

B _____ ? Did you get the letter?

A No, it was a scam.

B _____ !

3

B Have you reported it to the police?

A Yes, I have. They told me that hundreds of people have been tricked.

B _____ !

3 🔊 **31** **Listen to the conversation between Kate and the police officer. Then answer the questions.**

1 Who stole Kate's bag?

_____

2 What did Kate say the girl looked like?

_____

3 Where was Kate's bag when it was stolen?

_____

4 What did the police officer advise Kate not to do?

_____

5 Why did the police officer tell Kate she should be careful with her bag?

_____

6 What did Kate say was in her bag?

_____

DIALOGUE

1 **Complete the mini dialogues. Use phrases in the list.**

Tell me | No way | You'll never guess what | Really
There was a story | You won't believe what happened to
That's awful | I heard a really sad story | What

1

A _____ !

B _____ ?

A I've won a short story writing competition.

B That's amazing. Well done.

2

C _____ yesterday.

D _____ .

C Old Mrs Price's cat disappeared last week and now Mrs Price has died.

D _____ !

3

E _____ me last night.

F What?

E I fell asleep on the train and I didn't wake up until it got to London.

F _____ ! That's a long way from Oxford.

4

G _____ in the paper the other day about our art teacher.

H _____ ?

G Yes, apparently his grandfather was a famous artist. There's an exhibition of his paintings at the city centre art gallery next week.

2 **Write a short account of a time when you or someone you know had something stolen or was pickpocketed.**

Where were you / they? Who took it? What did they take?

Pronunciation

Intonation – expressing surprise
Go to page 120. 🔊

Writing part 2

1 Read the exam task. <u>Underline</u> the most important information.

Writing an email

You get an email from a friend. This friend has heard from another friend that your bike has been stolen. Write a reply. It must start with the following sentence:

Great to hear from you, and thanks for your concern.

In your email, you must:

- explain how you felt about your bike being stolen.
- agree that you should report it to the police.

Write your email in 140–190 words.

---

2 Read Anya's answer to the task. What part of the question does she fail to answer?

⊖ ☐ ✕

Great to hear from you, and thanks for your concern. Of course, I was very puzzled when I got to the bike rack and couldn't find my bike. Then I felt angry with the thief. How was I going to get home? I didn't have any money on me and it would take me ages to walk. Luckily I had my mobile phone with me, so I rang my mum and explained to her what had happened. She told me to wait there and she'd come and pick me up. She said we could go together and report it to the head teacher.

It's annoying because three other people have had their bikes stolen too, and that's just in the last week! I really hope the school will do something about it.

Oh – I'm sorry I have to go now. The police are here. The headmaster called them. I'll email you again later to let you know what they say.

Bye

Anya

---

3 Look at the questions Anya asked herself before writing her email. Use the email to find the answers to the questions.

1 How did I feel when I first realised the bike was missing?

2 Then, when I realised it had been stolen, how did I feel?

3 How else could I get home?

4 Who could come to help me?

5 Who should I report the theft to?

Exam guide: writing an email

Refer back to the exam guide in Unit 4, page 43

- Think carefully about who you are writing to. This will affect the kind of language you should use.
- You often have to report an event or something someone said in an email. Think about the reporting verbs you can use such as: *agree*, *explain* and *recommend*.
- Think about how you will start the email and how you will close it.

---

4 Read the task. Plan and then write your answer in 140–190 words.

You have been mugged. Write an email to a friend thanking him / her for an email he / she wrote to you expressing his / her concern. Explain what happened.

In your email you must say:

- Your wallet / purse was taken leaving you with no money to get home.
- You didn't report the incident to the police.
- Your mugger felt sorry for you and gave the purse / wallet back.

---

5 Ask a friend to read your story and complete the sentences about it.

I thought / didn't think the email explained everything

You could improve it by

CONSOLIDATION

LISTENING

1 ◀)) 34 Listen and (circle) A, B or C.

1   How many times has the boy's bike been stolen?
   A   two times in two years
   B   three times in two years
   C   two times in three years

2   Where was the bike stolen from?
   A   outside a shop
   B   in a shopping centre
   C   outside a shopping centre

3   Why is the boy going to the police station now?
   A   to give the police a description of his bike
   B   to collect his bike
   C   to see if the bike they found is really his or not

2 ◀)) 34 Listen again and complete with between two and four words.

1   The boy got the money to buy his bike by cutting _____ cars.

2   The boy had _____ on it but the thieves cut it off.

3   His bike was stolen in _____ .

4   The boy doesn't think they're _____ his bike.

5   The police have got _____ station that fits the boy's description.

GRAMMAR

3 (Circle) the correct options.

1   She told me *to leave / leave* right away.

2   We aren't *allow / allowed* to go in there without permission.

3   I don't think I'll ever get used to *drive / driving* on the left.

4   Does your school *make / let* you wear anything you want?

5   Lots of people don't like the weather here, but they soon *are / get* used to it.

6   I never want to get up at six o'clock, but my parents *let / make* me.

7   He asked me where *I was from / was I from*.

8   They encouraged us to *take / taking* to the exam.

9   I invited her *to come / come* with us.

10   She asked us what *did we have / we had* to do.

4 Rewrite the sentences using the correct form of the word in brackets.

0   My dad says I have to get up at 7.00. (make)
   My dad makes me get up at 7.00.

1   Our teacher says it's OK to use a dictionary. (let)
   Our teacher _____ .

2   We can't go into that room. (allowed)
   We _____ .

3   The headteacher told us to clean the playground. (make)
   The headteacher _____ .

4   Last week our mum said we couldn't watch TV. (let)
   Our mum _____ .

VOCABULARY

5 Complete with the correct particle.

1   Yesterday I just hung _____ with my friends.

2   Could you look _____ my cat while I'm away at the weekend?

3   What time does the plane take _____ ?

4   He decided to take _____ the piano when he was sixty.

5   We've always got _____ well together.

6   We didn't want to stop, so we just carried _____ walking.

7   I waited for hours but she didn't show _____ .

8   It's been ten years since my dad gave _____ smoking.

6 Complete each sentence with one word.

1   If you break that window you'll get into _____ with the neighbours.

2   I don't mind what we listen to. It's all the _____ to me.

3   Mum had to pay a _____ because she parked in the wrong place.

4   I don't know anyone who has ever _____ a crime.

5   She stole some money and went to _____ for three months.

6   There was a _____ in at the supermarket. The thieves stole a lot of food and money.

7   He was found guilty and the judge gave him a life _____ .

8   Hey, stop asking me that question! _____ and for all, I don't know!

9   He always says 'please' and 'thank you', he's so _____ .

10   She only thinks about herself. She's really _____ .

DIALOGUE

7 **Complete the conversation with the phrases in the list.**

point | don't mention it | I'm with you | it in one
I know how you feel | in fact | get me wrong | be honest

SANDRA   Here's your satnav back. Thanks a lot for lending it to me.

JASON   [1]_____ . I hope it was useful.

SANDRA   Yes, it was thanks. But listen, Jason – Don't [2]_____ , but maybe you should get a new one.

JASON   Why? Is it out of date?

SANDRA   Yes! Got [3]_____ . I mean, it was useful, like I said. But three times it tried to make us drive the wrong way down a one-way street. I guess they changed the directions but the satnav didn't know that.

JASON   So [4]_____ , I don't need a new satnav – I just need to update the map.

SANDRA   Well, to [5]_____ , that's not the only problem. The display is a bit old-fashioned, too.

JASON   Yeah, good [6]_____ . And the battery isn't very good either, is it?

SANDRA   No. So really it all adds up to just one thing – buy a new one!

JASON   Yeah, [7]_____ on that. I just haven't got any money right now so it's going to have to wait.

SANDRA   Yes, [8]_____ . I spent all my money over the weekend. Well, see you!

READING

8 **Read the stories and answer the questions.**

STORY 1

1   Why was the woman crying when the police officer arrived?

_____

2   What had the woman and boyfriend done, and why?

_____

3   How did Officer Meharu know that the burglary was not real?

_____

STORY 2

4   Why did the boy take out his mobile phone?

_____

5   What did the thief upload onto WhatsApp?

_____

6   What was hard for the police to believe?

_____

WRITING

9 **Find an example of another dumb criminal and write the story. Write about 150–200 words.**

Dumb criminals

[1] In 2010, police in Calgary, Canada got a call from a woman who said that her home had been burgled. Jewellery was missing, all the home electronics like the TV and DVD player were gone, windows had been smashed, and so on. It isn't surprising that the woman was crying when the police officer arrived. The officer was 37-year-old Charanjit Meharu, who is of Indian origin.

While Officer Meharu was checking the crime scene, the woman's phone rang. It was her father, and she began to tell her father – speaking in French – that it wasn't a real burglary: she and her boyfriend had hidden the things, broken the window, and made up the whole story in order to get money from the insurance company.

What the woman didn't know is that Officer Meharu speaks seven languages: English, Punjabi, Hindi, Urdu, Arabic, Gujarati – and French.

[2] In 2013, a man in Essex, England stopped a 12-year-old boy in the street and asked him the time. The boy took out his mobile phone, and the man grabbed it and ran away. Unfortunately this kind of mobile phone theft happens a lot – but what happened next doesn't happen very often.

The thief, who was described by police as being in his early 20s and about 1.6 metres tall, used the stolen phone to take two selfies, which he then uploaded onto WhatsApp. This immediately sent a notification to the mother of the boy who owned the phone. The man also used instant messaging to tell the world that he lives in South London.

The police said it was hard to believe that a thief would do something to tell the world about his crime, and who he was. They arrested him soon after.

9 | WHAT HAPPENED?

GRAMMAR
Modals of deduction (present) `SB page 86`

1 ★☆☆ (Circle) the correct words.

1 They could be Colombian because they're speaking *Spanish / German*.

2 It can't be a spider; it's only got *six / eight* legs.

3 Oliver must really love that film. He's seen it *once / ten times*.

4 Dana can't know what the homework is. She *was / wasn't* at school yesterday.

5 Jo must travel a lot. Her passport's full of *visa stamps / blank pages*.

6 Bernie might be tired. She's been *working hard / doing nothing* all day.

7 They might not speak English. They're *French / American*.

8 Dave must like One Direction. He's got *all / none* of their CDs.

2 ★★☆ Complete the conversation with *must / can't / might*.

RUTH Look, Claudia Jones is on Facebook. I'm going to send her a friend request. There – done.

IAN Wow, she's got five hundred friends. She ¹_____ be really popular.

RUTH Well they ²_____ all be real friends. No one can have that many. Not even Claudia.

IAN That's true. She ³_____ not really know most of them.

RUTH Yes, twenty proper friends at the most. The rest of them ⁴_____ just be friends of friends. She probably just accepts anyone who wants to be her friend.

IAN Why does she do that?

RUTH I don't know. She ⁵_____ just be a bit lonely. Maybe it makes her feel better.

IAN But that ⁶_____ work. Having lots of false friends doesn't make anyone feel better.

RUTH Oh look. She ⁷_____ be online because she's replied to my request already.

IAN And what does she say?

RUTH I ⁸_____ believe it. She said 'no'!

should(n't) have `SB page 87`

3 ★☆☆ Complete the sentences with phrases in the list.

shouldn't go | should invite | should have watched
should have invited | should watch | shouldn't say
shouldn't have said | shouldn't have gone

1 The game last night was brilliant. You _____ it.

2 That old house looks really dangerous. My mum says we _____ inside.

3 You _____ Joe. He'll be upset if you don't.

4 You _____ anything. It was our secret.

5 You _____ things if you don't really mean them.

6 There's a great film on TV tonight. You _____ it.

7 The party was really boring. We _____ .

8 You _____ Kate to your party. She was really upset that you didn't.

4 ★★☆ Read the story and complete the sentences with *should(n't) have* and a verb in the list.

~~take~~ | leave | go | wear | tell | charge

Gina went on a bike ride. After about 10 km she had a problem with her bike but she couldn't fix it because she had no tools with her. She took out her phone but she couldn't make a call because it had no battery left. She decided to get a bus home but when she looked for her purse it wasn't in her pocket. There was nothing she could do but walk. It started raining and she got really wet because she had no coat. Two hours later when she finally got home, her mum was really angry with her because she had been worried about her. It's the last time Gina is going on a bike ride.

0 She ***should have taken*** some tools with her.

1 She _____ her phone before leaving.

2 She _____ her purse at home.

3 She _____ a coat.

4 She _____ her mum where she was going.

5 She _____ on a bike ride!

5 ★★★ Complete the conversations with your own ideas. Use *should(n't) have.*

0 **A** I'm so tired today.
B *You should have gone to bed earlier.*

1 **A** This T-shirt is too small for me.
B _____

2 **A** Jim's really angry with me.
B _____

3 **A** I'm so full! I feel a bit sick.
B _____

4 **A** I haven't got enough money left to get the bus.
B _____

5 **A** I don't understand this homework at all.
B _____

Modals of deduction (past) [SB page 89]

6 ★☆☆ Match the sentences.

1 She must have been happy. ☐
2 She can't have been happy. ☐
3 She might have been happy. ☐
4 He must have been hungry. ☐
5 He can't have been hungry. ☐
6 He could have been hungry. ☐

a Her husband crashed her car again.
b He ate everything.
c But he was too polite to ask for any food.
d Her football team won the cup.
e He didn't eat anything.
f But it's always difficult to know what she's feeling.

7 ★★☆ Complete the text with the verbs in brackets and the correct modal verbs.

Police are still looking for the multi-millionaire banker Cecil Montgomery who disappeared from his home last week. At first they were sure criminals [1]_____ (take) him from the family home but now they are investigating the possibility that he [2]_____ (disappear) on purpose. It seems that he was having financial problems and owed a lot of people a lot of money and police believe that he [3]_____ (go) into hiding to escape from these people. One thing for sure is that he [4]_____ (leave) the country as police found his passport in his office desk. Police are now asking members of the public for their help. They feel certain that someone [5]_____ (see) Cecil in the last few days and they are asking that person to come forward and help them with their investigation.

8 ★★★ Complete the sentences with your own ideas. Use modals of deduction.

1 Our teacher looks really happy. He _____

2 I recognise his face. I'm sure _____

3 Nobody went to his party. He _____

4 I'm not sure how I fell off my bike. I _____

5 Our cat is missing. I'm worried _____

6 Jane is two hours late. _____

7 She fell asleep in two minutes. _____

8 She hasn't got any money. _____

GET IT RIGHT! 👁
Modals of deduction: past

Learners sometimes use *can have* for speculating about past events, whereas *could have* is required. But remember we use *can't have* in the negative.

✓ He **could have** known the truth.
✗ He ~~can have~~ known the truth.
✓ He **can't have** known the truth.

Choose the correct sentence from the pairs.

1 a It must be in the garage. It can have been put anywhere else.
b It must be in the garage. It can't have been put anywhere else.

2 a Do you think it could have been someone else?
b Do you think it can have been someone else?

3 a She can't have known about it because nobody told her.
b She could have known about it because nobody told her.

4 a I don't think we can have managed it without your help.
b I don't think we could have managed it without your help.

5 a They can't have got there in time. Their car was too slow.
b They could have got there in time. Their car was too slow.

6 a Could Carl have given the keys to his friend?
b Can Carl have given the keys to his friend?

VOCABULARY

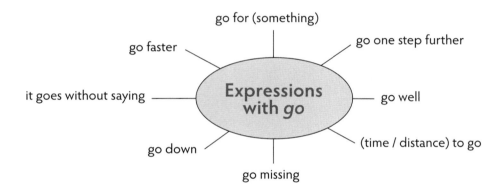

Key words in context

aviation	I'm really interested in **aviation**. I'd love to be a pilot one day.
civilisation	The Incas were an ancient **civilisation** that lived in central America.
evidence	The police know who robbed the bank but they haven't got any **evidence**.
genuine	I think this is a **genuine** Chinese vase from the 15th Century.
haunted	They say the house is **haunted** by a young woman who was killed in it.
monster	I love **monster** films like *Godzilla* and *King Kong*.
phenomenon	Crop circles are a strange **phenomenon** that some people think is linked to alien activity.
pioneering	My grandfather did a lot of **pioneering** work in the early days of the Internet. He was one of the first people to really develop it.
pyramid	I'd love to go to Cairo and see the **pyramids**.
spiral	We walked up and up the **spiral** staircase and finally arrived at the top of the tower.
spy on	I think Clara's **spying on** me. I see her everywhere I go.
suicide	The police say he committed **suicide** but I think he was murdered.
well	When we were young we had to get all our water from a **well** at the bottom of our garden.

Mysteries SB page 86

1 ★☆☆ **Find eight adjectives to describe a mystery and then write them below the wordsearch.**

U	A	J	U	B	M	I	O	X	P	E	S	I	F	O	U
W	N	J	R	E	A	W	C	B	X	I	J	A	L	P	T
T	U	E	G	U	Q	L	V	K	E	I	Z	X	S	M	Y
R	E	T	X	B	W	U	I	Q	A	C	V	E	U	N	G
T	Y	S	D	P	D	O	L	E	W	T	C	M	O	I	R
R	Y	B	E	U	L	Y	C	E	N	R	I	O	I	Q	A
B	N	M	R	Z	W	A	C	O	E	P	L	A	R	A	S
Y	U	B	N	Z	R	E	I	T	Q	C	M	T	E	C	X
M	N	B	L	L	I	Y	M	N	Q	O	A	P	T	L	K
K	L	J	U	I	O	L	I	P	E	D	X	M	S	Q	A
Z	V	B	E	N	W	Q	I	L	K	D	N	O	Y	M	L
W	I	Y	E	G	N	A	R	T	S	N	O	D	M	D	C
C	U	P	W	O	L	O	O	H	M	B	W	B	B	X	U
I	L	L	A	W	Q	M	V	C	X	R	E	T	I	H	G
E	X	T	R	A	T	E	R	R	E	S	T	R	I	A	L

1 _____

2 _____

3 _____

4 _____

5 _____

6 _____

7 _____

8 _____

2 ★★☆ (Circle) **the correct words.**

1 Hannah hasn't returned my call, which is really *strange / unexplained*.

2 I didn't really understand the end of the film. It was a bit *secret / puzzling*.

3 Scientists believe the object is *odd / alien* and from another planet.

4 I don't want you to tell anyone. It's top *puzzling / secret*.

5 Anna's acting a bit *alien / mysterious*. I think she might have a new boyfriend.

6 I'm sure I had a £10 note in my wallet but it's not here. That's *secret / odd*.

7 I didn't like that man. He was very *extraterrestrial / strange*.

8 I went to the party dressed as an *extraterrestrial / odd*.

9 To this day, the disappearance of our neighbour is still *alien / unexplained*.

10 Some people claim Roswell was a *secret / puzzling* military operation.

Expressions with *go* SB page 89

3 ★☆☆ **Match the sentence halves and then match with the pictures.**

1 I don't think the party's ☐

2 Mum's gone one step further ☐

3 Strange – my sandwich ☐

4 I think it goes without saying ☐

5 It doesn't go any ☐

6 Come on – only ☐

a has gone missing.

b faster, I'm afraid.

c 50 km to go.

d with your cake this year.

e going so well.

f that you're not coming in here.

 A ☐
 B ☐
 C ☐

 D ☐
 E ☐
 F ☐

4 ★★☆ **Complete the conversations with the expressions in the list.**

for | one step further | a bit faster | without saying
really well | down | 5 km to | missing

1 A Come on, Dad. Can't you go _____ ?
   B No, I can't. And what's the big hurry anyway?

2 A Are we nearly there yet?
   B Nearly. We've just got _____ go.

3 A How was the exam?
   B It went _____ . I think I've passed.

4 A Do you want to try again to lift 100 kg?
   B I think I'll go _____ and try 110 kg.

5 A Is there any news on that yacht that went _____ last night?
   B No, there's still no sign of it anywhere.

6 A Did you see where my kite went _____ ?
   B I think it was somewhere in that field over there.

7 A Have you decided what to eat?
   B I think I'll go _____ the steak, please.

8 A So are you going to invite me to your party?
   B Of course – it goes _____ . You are my best friend after all.

READING

1 REMEMBER AND CHECK Match the numbers to what they describe. Then check your answers in the article on page 85 of the Student's Book.

1	a hundred	a	The age of Teotihuacan.
2	three hundred thousand	b	The number of dogs that have died at the Overtoun Bridge in the last half century.
3	over two thousand	c	The age of the Lolladoff plate.
4	fifty	d	The age of the Nampa doll.
5	twelve thousand	e	How far the Nampa doll was found under the earth.

2 Read the article. What sort of animals do the Nazca lines show? _____

Solving the World Mysteries with Science:
THE NAZCA LINES OF PERU

The Nazca Lines in Peru are huge pictures that were drawn into the ground by digging shallow lines into the earth. The lines take away the red stone which covers the surface leaving the white rock below exposed. An area of 190 square miles in the Nazca desert in Southern Peru is covered by these simple pictures, which include birds, spiders, fish and sharks. Some of these pictures are nearly 200 metres wide.

What's so mysterious about these lines? Well, although they date back to between 400 and 650 AD, they were only discovered in the 1930s. The reason for this is that the pictures only become clear when they are seen from the air. So it was only when aeroplanes started flying over the area that people realised what they were. Of course, this led to the question: how did these pictures get there all those years ago? How could these people have made such drawings without the ability to fly? Or did they have the ability to fly? Author Jim Woodman suggested that the Nazca people could have invented simple hot-air balloons and used them to produce the art. He even built a working balloon using materials they would have had. Not many people were convinced by his ideas though. Other people suggested the lines might be extraterrestrial, that they were the work of aliens visiting our Earth. More and more theories were offered and one of the great modern mysteries was born.

However, when some wooden sticks were found in the ground in the area and carbon-dated, it showed that they were from the same age as the drawings. Some scientists suggested that the Nazca people might have put these sticks in the ground to help them with the drawings. By placing the sticks in the correct positions and connecting them with long ropes, the Nazca people could have used them to draw the lines to make the pictures. One scientist, Dr. Joe Nickell of the University of Kentucky was so sure that this was the answer that he decided to try and show how it could be done. Using only tools that the Nazca might have had he set about trying to draw a huge picture of a bird on a piece of land. With a few friends it took him a few hours to produce a perfect Nazca picture and show how these pictures probably got there.

3 Read the article again and answer the questions.

1 How were the lines drawn?

_____

2 When and how were the pictures discovered?

_____

3 What is Jim Woodman's theory?

_____

4 What did he do to try and prove it?

_____

5 How does Joe Nickell believe the lines were made?

_____

6 What did he do to prove these ideas?

_____

Pronunciation
Moving word stress
Go to page 120.

DEVELOPING WRITING

A blog entry about a mystery

1 Read the blog entry. What does the writer think about the Bélmez faces? Tick a box.

☐ They were fake.   ☐ They were real.

What do you think?

☐ They were fake.   ☐ They were real.

[A] On the 23rd August 1971, María Gómez Cámara saw a human face appear on the kitchen floor of her home in the southern Spanish town of Bélmez. So she told her husband and son, who, **[B]** broke up the kitchen floor and laid down another. However when a second face appeared sometime after, word got out to the mayor of Bélmez. He ordered that the floor should be cut out and taken away for study.

Ever since these initial sightings, there have been a number of reports of the sudden appearance and disappearances of human faces in the kitchen floor. **[C]** tourists have visited La Casa de las Caras (The House of the Faces) hoping to experience the phenomena for themselves.

Of course, several theories were put forward to try and explain what was going on. One idea was that María herself could have produced the faces through a process called 'thoughtography', in which María was subconsciously projecting the pictures onto the floor from her mind.

Other people looked for a more scientific explanation and a lot of testing was done on the chemicals in the concrete. Studies showed that the images might have formed through chemical reactions. This could have been a natural process or it could have been done deliberately.

[D] I think the faces were made by María's husband or son. **[E]** To make a lot of money perhaps. **[F]** What about you?

---

2 Blogs are often quite informal and chatty in their style. Where do these informal phrases fit into the text?

1 I'm not a big believer in paranormal activity and ☐

2 Why? ☐

3 One of the weirdest things I've ever heard about are the Bélmez faces. ☐

4 Well that's what I think. ☐

5 probably not being too happy about it, ☐

6 Millions of ☐

3 Match the phrases in Exercise 2 with the effect they have.

a A way of introducing your own opinion ☐

b A way of summing up your thoughts ☐

c Using a question which you answer yourself to say what you think ☐

d Using a superlative to introduce the topic in a dramatic way ☐

e Exaggeration ☐

f Imagining / supposing how someone must have felt ☐

4 Do some research about a famous mystery from your country. Make notes and write an entry for a blog in about 250 words.

- What is the mystery?
- What are the theories around it?
- Do I believe it?

_____

_____

_____

_____

_____

_____

CHECKLIST ✔

☐ Explain the story behind it.

☐ Discuss some of the theories about it. Don't forget to use modals of deduction.

☐ Use informal language to make your blog more interesting.

☐ Say what you think.

☐ Include a short survey for your readers to answer.

LISTENING

1 🔊 **37** Listen to two short conversations and answer the questions.

1 What does Jennie want for her birthday?

_____

2 What did Sean find in the fields?

_____

2 🔊 **37** Listen again and answer the questions.

CONVERSATION 1

1 Why is Lisa angry with Ollie?

_____

2 What suggestion does Ollie make?

_____

3 What does Lisa think of his suggestion?

_____

CONVERSATION 2

4 What was Sean doing when he found something?

_____

5 What does his mum tell him he should have done?

_____

6 What is she going to do now?

_____

DIALOGUE

1 Complete these parts of the conversations with *should(n't) have* and a verb in the list.

leave | tell | do | take

1

OLLIE I just asked what present I should bring her.
She wants a book.

LISA I can't believe you told her. You
¹_____ that. It was
supposed to be
a surprise.

OLLIE Well you ²_____ me that.

LISA I did but obviously you weren't listening …
again!

2

MUM This is really old. It could be really important.

SEAN You think?

MUM Yes, you ³_____ it. You
⁴_____ it where it was
and called the museum.

SEAN Why? I found it. It's mine.

2 Put the missing lines in the correct places to make three short dialogues.

DIALOGUE 1

PAUL Have you seen the TV remote, Alex?

ALEX _____

PAUL _____

ALEX _____

PAUL |_____

DIALOGUE 2

DANA Any news from the police on the missing
Picasso painting?

FOX _____

DANA _____

FOX _____

DANA _____

DIALOGUE 3

LUCY My bike. Someone's stolen it!

JACK _____

LUCY _____

JACK _____

LUCY _____

1 So try the dog basket – Spike might have taken it.

2 Stolen it. Are you sure?

3 Well it was long enough for them to break the lock.
I don't believe it!

4 Well, let's hope they arrest someone soon and find
the painting.

5 I think it must have been someone who worked at
the gallery.

6 Of course I'm sure. I left it locked up just here.

7 That's a good idea. I'll go and have a look.

8 No, I haven't. It's probably down the side of the
sofa. That's where it usually is.

9 They can't have gone far; we were only in the shop
five minutes.

10 I've already searched the whole sofa. It's not there.

11 No, they don't even know how the robber got into
the building.

12 Yes, I think you're right. Someone who knew how
to turn off the alarm.

3 Choose one of the lines below and use it to start
or end a five line dialogue.

1 You shouldn't have done that!

2 You should have told me straight away.

3 It must have been Paul.

4 It can't have been easy.

Listening part 2

Exam guide: sentence completion

In part 2 of the listening exam, you will listen to a monologue (one person speaking) or a recording with two or more speakers lasting around three minutes. To answer the questions, you have to complete the sentences using the information you hear in the recording.

- You will be given plenty of time to read through the questions first. Read the sentences to help you prepare yourself for some of the things you will hear.

- Underline some of the key words in each of the sentences. This will help you focus on the important parts of the listening.

- The focus of this listening test is on detail, and to answer the questions correctly you will need to identify specific information. You should write the word(s) exactly as you hear them in the recording.

- The monologue can be quite long, so try to stay focussed. If you lose your place, remember that the questions are in the same order as the information in the recording, so concentrate on answering the next question.

- Use your second listening to focus on the answers you didn't get the first time round and to check the answers you did get.

- The answers tend to be a single word and you will rarely need to write more than three.

1 🔊 **38** **You will hear Gaby talking about an unforgettable school trip to the ancient monument of Stonehenge in South West England. For questions 1–10, complete the sentences with a word or short phrase.**

Gaby and her classmates spent most of their time in **(1)** ＿＿＿＿＿＿ on their UK holiday.

The first thing that impressed her about Stonehenge was the **(2)** ＿＿＿＿＿＿ of it.

It's estimated that work started on Stonehenge **(3)** ＿＿＿＿＿ years ago.

The stones that were used in the **(4)** ＿＿＿＿＿＿ of construction came from mountains about 240 miles away.

The heaviest stone in the monument weighs **(5)** ＿＿＿＿＿＿ tonnes.

To move the largest of the stones you would need a total of **(6)** ＿＿＿＿＿＿ men.

Gaby says that the difference between Stonehenge and **(7)** ＿＿＿＿＿＿ is that we can't be sure why it was built.

Some people say it was built to study the **(8)** ＿＿＿＿＿＿ in the night sky.

Gaby doesn't believe the stones were put there by **(9)** ＿＿＿＿＿.

Gaby bought a **(10)** ＿＿＿＿＿＿ to remind her of her visit to Stonehenge.

---

10 MONEY

GRAMMAR

Future continuous `SB page 94`

1 ★ ☆ ☆ **Put the words in order to make sentences. Put the verbs in the future continuous.**

This time next year, …

0 my / present / cookery show / grandma / on TV / a
my grandma will be presenting a cookery show on TV.

1 dad / my / race / the / in / Grand Prix

2 sister / work / children's home / Cambodia / in / my / at / a

3 brother / my / sail / world / the / around

4 mum / act / my / in / a / production / theatre

5 cousin / research / my / cancer / cure / a / for

6 best friend / trek / Africa / round / my

7 I / human rights / a / lawyer / famous / work / as

2 ★ ★ ★ **What do you think will be happening fifty years from now? Use the ideas in brackets to write sentences in the future continuous.**

0 (type of transport / travel)
People will be travelling in computer-controlled flying cars.

1 (phones / use)

2 (money / use)

3 (school text books / use)

4 (houses / live)

3 ★ ★ ★ **Write fantasy predictions for your friends and family. Use the future continuous.**

Ten years from now, …

1 my _____

2 my _____

3 my _____

4 my _____

5 my _____

6 I _____

Future perfect `SB page 97`

4 ★ ☆ ☆ **Complete the conversation with the future perfect tense of the verbs in brackets.**

MUM Have you done your homework yet?

JOE No, but I ¹_____ (finish) it by the time Dad gets home.

MUM Have you tidied your room yet?

JOE No, but I ²_____ (tidy) it by bedtime.

MUM Have you fed the cat yet?

JOE No, but I ³_____ (feed) it by 6 pm.

MUM Have you done that essay yet?

JOE No, but I ⁴_____ (write) it by the time it's due in.

MUM And have you finished dinner yet?

JOE No, but I ⁵_____ (eat) it by the time you've finished yours.

5 ★★☆ Complete the conversation with the future perfect of the verbs in the list.

become | finish | buy | see | travel | swim
not have | cycle | move | go | sail | find

MATT   What plans have you got for the future, Matilda?

MATILDA Me? By 2030, I [1]_____ university, and I [2]_____ to New York. I [3]_____ an amazing apartment there, and I [4]_____ a successful architect.

MATT   Wow!

MATILDA What about you? [5]_____ you _____ round the world? You always said you'd like to do that.

MATT   Of course. I [6]_____ across the English Channel, and I [7]_____ across the Atlantic Ocean. I [8]_____ across China, and I [9]_____ the pyramids in Mexico and Guatemala. Oh, and of course, I [10]_____ kayaking down the Grand Canyon.

MATILDA [11]_____ a job?

MATT   No, I [12]_____ time to find a job!

Future perfect and future continuous

6 ★★☆ Complete the predictions with the future perfect or the future continuous.

1 By 2020, internet use _____ (reach) 5 billion worldwide.
2 By 2030, smoking in public _____ (be) banned in every US state.
3 By 2040, robots _____ (fight) on the battlefields instead of humans.
4 By 2050, people _____ (use) virtual telepathy in personal communications.
5 By 2060, nearly half the Amazon rainforest _____ (be) cut down.
6 By 2070, soldiers in the military _____ (wear) invisibility suits.
7 By 2080, people _____ (drive) flying cars.
8 By 2090, many of the world's languages _____ (disappear).

7 ★★☆ Use the future perfect or the future continuous tense, and a verb from the list, to complete the text.

~~travel~~ | live | settle | build | eat | become | develop

By 2050, I don't think people [0] *will have travelled* to Mars. However, I think they [1]_____ in space. Some people [2]_____ in space stations, because the Earth [3]_____ too crowded.
I think scientists [4]_____ huge farms in space in special glass buildings, and they [5]_____ a very healthy diet for people. People [6]_____ specially developed fruit and vegetables.

8 ★★★ Write goals for yourself. Complete the sentences using the future perfect or future continuous.

1 By tomorrow evening, I _____
_____
2 By next week, _____
_____
3 By next year, _____
_____
4 By the time I'm twenty, _____
_____
5 By the time I'm fifty, _____
_____

GET IT RIGHT!
Future perfect vs. future simple

Learners often confuse the future perfect with the future simple.

✓ *By the end of next year, I **will have finished** my studies.*
✗ *By the end of next year, I ~~will finish~~ my studies.*

Complete the sentences with the verb in brackets in the correct form: future perfect or future simple.

0 I *will have come* back to Beijing by June. (come)
1 We hope you _____ to our party next weekend. (come)
2 I'd really like that game – maybe my dad _____ it for me. (buy)
3 By the time I finish my English course, my skills _____ a lot. (improve)
4 I promise I _____ there at 5 pm tomorrow. (be)
5 We hope that in a week's time we _____ all our work. (finish)
6 By this time tomorrow they _____ in Australia. (arrive)

VOCABULARY

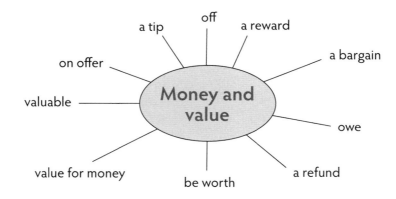

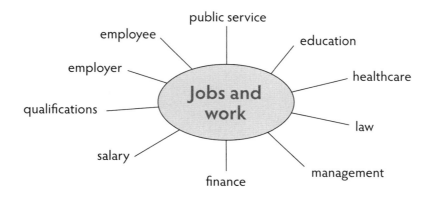

by

by some people	the person / people who do something
by solving	a way to do something
by the shoe shop	a location
by tomorrow	a time in the future

Key words in context

banknote	I didn't have any change so I had to buy my chewing gum using a £20 **banknote**.
coin	This machine doesn't take 50p **coins**.
currency	The Euro is the **currency** of the European Union.
invention	Bitcoin is the most amazing **invention**.
monetary system	Bitcoin is a great alternative **monetary system** to credit cards.
predict	Who can **predict** when people will stop using regular money?
same as usual	I'll have the **same as usual**: coffee with milk, and a bit of sugar.
sponsorship	After getting **sponsorship** from their university, the students could afford to start work on their new project.

Money and value `SB page 94`

1 ★★★ **Complete the sentences with the words in the list. There are three you won't use.**

worth | valuable | bargain | owe | refund
value for money | tip | on offer | reward

1 This ruby ring is quite _____ . My great-grandmother gave it to my mum.

2 Some of my granddad's stamps are _____ a lot of money now.

3 I _____ Jack some money. I borrowed ten pounds from him last week.

4 These trainers are usually over fifty pounds. I got them for twenty pounds. They were a real _____ .

5 We got the concert tickets half price. I think they are very good _____ .

6 The shop owner gave me a _____ for catching the shoplifter.

Jobs and work `SB page 97`

2 ★☆☆ (Circle) **the correct words to complete the conversations.**

1 My dad works in *healthcare / finance*. He's a nurse.

2 What *sponsorship / qualifications* do you need to be an air traffic controller?

3 I've been an *employee / employer* of SmartArt for ten years now.

4 Mr Brown is my *employer / employee*. I've worked for his company for fifteen years now.

5 Pete's got a *finance / management* job now; he's got a team of people working under him.

6 There are a lot of companies offering *education / sponsorship*. You could apply to a few of them and see what happens.

3 ★★☆ **Match the sentences.**

1 I work for a bank. ☐
2 I work as a consultant in a hospital. ☐
3 I am a head teacher at a primary school in North London. ☐
4 I'm paid by the government. ☐
5 I want to be a high court judge. ☐

a I work in education.
b I work in public services.
c I work in finance.
d I'm studying law at university.
e I work in healthcare.

4 ★★★ **Unscramble the words in brackets to complete the sentences. Then match the answers to the questions.**

1 Where were the first _____ made? (noics) ☐

2 Where was the first _____ made? (kanb toen) ☐

3 Whose portrait is on more _____ than any other person? (rruceniesc) ☐

4 What were the first _____? (kanbs) ☐

5 What kind of money do they _____ we will be using in the future? (dictpre) ☐

a Queen Elizabeth II.
b They were grain warehouses in Assyria and Babylonia.
c They were made in the ancient kingdom of Lydia.
d It was made in China.
e We'll all be using Bitcoins.

Wordwise `SB page 99`

by

5 **Read the four sentences. In which sentence is *by* used:**

1 to say how something is done? ☐
2 to say where something is? ☐
3 to say when something is done? ☐
4 to say who does something? ☐

a There's no traffic today, so I think we'll get there **by** ten o'clock.

b I bought these shoes at that new shop **by** the supermarket.

c This photo was taken **by** my grandmother.

d I bought my new computer **by** saving money for six months!

6 **Complete the sentences with the phrases in the list.**

by working | by a friend | by ten o'clock
by my bedroom door | by Monday | by practising

1 This book was written _____ of my parents.

2 We've got three days to do the homework – the teacher said he wants it _____ .

3 I learned to play the guitar _____ two hours every day.

4 Jack made some money _____ in a café at the weekends.

5 Our cat always sleeps _____ .

6 The film starts at 8 pm, so I'm sure it will have finished _____ .

READING

1 **REMEMBER AND CHECK** Match the sentence halves. Then check your answers in the article on page 93 of the Student's Book.

1 In a few decades' time,
2 Some people have already called the Bitcoin
3 'Mining' is a way of earning Bitcoins
4 An IT expert, James Howell, lost his Bitcoin fortune
5 The recycling centre told James that if he wanted to find his hard disk
6 James has offered a reward

a by solving very complicated mathematical problems.
b when he threw away an old hard disk on which he had stored them.
c he would have to search through an area one metre deep and as big as a football pitch.
d to anyone who can find his hard disk.
e we will all be paying with the same currency – the Bitcoin.
f the 'gold' of the Internet.

2 Read the article quickly and answer the questions.

1 Who was the first person to have his portrait on a coin?

    _____

2 Which phrase has its origins in Viking times?

    _____

WORDS ABOUT MONEY

Money has been around for 12,000 years. The oldest money ever found were some coins made of obsidian, which is a dark glass-like volcanic rock. The obsidian coins were found in what is now modern day Turkey. Paper money has been around since the 9th Century AD. It was invented in China and it was called 'flying money' because it would blow away in the wind.

So money has been around for centuries, but have you ever wondered why we call it money? The answer is that the Romans made their coins in the temple of Juno Moneta, who was the goddess of marriage and women. The word 'money' comes from the name 'Moneta'. Did you know the word in English for 'to manufacture coins' is 'mint' and that also comes from 'Moneta'?

In fact, the Romans were the first to stamp a face on a coin. And can you guess who that famous Roman was? Yes, it was the great Roman Emperor, Julius Caesar. He had just won a war, and he decided that he would reward himself by putting his portrait on the coins.

'Cash' is another term we use for money. It comes from the ancient Chinese word for a bundle of coins. The Chinese used to carry their coins on strings. One hundred coins on a string was called one 'cash'. The Chinese may have got the word from the Portuguese who called their coins 'caixa', which is pronounced 'cash-a'.

When someone loses all their money they become 'bankrupt', and the origin of that word is the Italian phrase 'banca rotta', which means 'broken bench'. In the years of early banking, people who exchanged and lent money did their business in the marketplace at a bench. If the man at the bench, or the 'banker', ran out of money or was unfair, his bench would be broken.

Another term we use when talking about money is 'to pay through the nose'. If we say 'he paid through the nose' we mean that he paid a high price for something. That phrase has its origins in Viking times. The Vikings asked for a reward for not raiding a town. If the king refused to pay the reward, his nose was cut off. In other words, the king paid through the nose. Money has been around for centuries and the words we use have been around for centuries too.

3 Read the article again and answer the questions.

1 Where was the oldest money found?
2 Which word originates from the name of a Roman goddess?
3 How many Chinese coins made one 'cash'?
4 Which language does the word 'cash' probably originate from?
5 When would the Italians break the 'banker's' bench?
6 What does 'to pay through the nose' mean?

4 Do some research on the Internet to find the origins of the word 'salary'. Then write a short paragraph about it.

DEVELOPING WRITING

An essay about the importance of money

1 Read Matt's essay for the title 'Money is not the most important thing in the world' and answer the questions.

1 Is the style formal or informal? _____

2 Is it a balanced argument, i.e. are there arguments for and against the statement? _____

> My dad earned a huge salary and he had a very successful career, but we never saw him. For me, money is not the most important thing in the world.
>
> Firstly, some people earn a lot of money but they don't have time to spend it because they are working so hard. [1]Secondly, they spend long hours in an office, so they don't have time to see family or friends.
>
> [2]Without doubt, there is a feeling of safety in being wealthy. You will never be homeless or hungry. You will be able to buy your children everything they want. In addition, you will probably have reached the top of your career and you will have achieved success as well as wealth, but will you be happy? Furthermore, will your family be happy?
>
> On the one hand, money makes you rich, but on the other hand, it makes you poor. You are able to buy your children everything they want. [3]However, you can't give them all the time and love they want. [4]For this reason, I conclude that money is definitely not the most important thing in the world.

2 Match the underlined words and phrases with the similar phrases below. Then find two other examples in the essay of ways to link ideas.

but ☐   furthermore ☐   therefore ☐   without question ☐   _____ _____

3 Number the statements in the correct order for an essay plan:

Matt's plan for his essay

☐ Present my first argument against the statement.

☐ State whether I am 'for' or 'against' the argument in the introductory paragraph.

☐ Present my first argument for the statement.

☐ Conclude the essay.

☐ Present my second argument against the statement.

☐ Present my second argument for the statement.

4 Now plan your essay. Write two statements to support your argument, two statements against and a conclusion.

Paragraph plan	Money is important	Money isn't important
First		
Second		
Conclusion		

5 Now write your essay. Write between 200–250 words.

- Look at the vocabulary in the unit to see what words you could use.
- Check with your paragraph plan, and make sure you give arguments for and against.
- Make sure you mention your opinion, and use the last lines to sum up and state your conclusion.

CHECKLIST ✓

☐ Money and work vocabulary

☐ Arguments for

☐ Arguments against

☐ My opinion

☐ Conclusion

LISTENING

1 🔊 39 Listen to the conversation. What do Melissa and Matt think they'll be doing in ten years' time?

_____

2 🔊 39 Listen again. Mark the sentences T (true) or F (false).

1 Melissa and Matt start talking about the past. ☐

2 Melissa wants to work in healthcare. ☐

3 Melissa doesn't think she's clever enough to become a lawyer. ☐

4 Money isn't important to Matt. ☐

5 Matt doesn't want to work in finance because it isn't creative enough. ☐

6 Melissa pays for the coffee and cakes. ☐

DIALOGUE

1 🔊 39 Listen again and complete these parts of the conversation.

1

MATT   So what are you going to have?

MELISSA   ¹_____ . Coffee and a slice of cheesecake.

MATT   Two coffees, a slice of cheesecake and a slice of ²_____ , please.

WAITER   No problem.

2

MATT   So, Melissa, what do you think you'll be doing in ten years' time? No don't answer. Let me guess. I think you ³_____ in healthcare. You'll be a nurse or maybe even a surgeon.

MELISSA   No way! I feel sick when I see blood.

MATT   ⁴_____ ! You'd make a brilliant nurse.

3

MELISSA   ⁵_____ . What about you? Money's important to you, isn't it? You'll probably be ⁶_____ finance.

MATT   No – too boring. I want to do something a bit creative.

4

MATT   ⁷_____ , Melissa. I haven't got any money as usual.

MELISSA   Never mind. ⁸_____ .

MATT   But you paid last time.

MELISSA   It doesn't matter. I can pay next time too.

MATT   ⁹_____ , I'll be paying for all the coffees. You'll see!

PHRASES FOR FLUENCY   SB page 99

1 Fill in the missing vowels to complete the phrases. Then match them to the expressions which are similar.

1 Th _t's _ sh_m_ . ☐

2 N_ v_ r m_nd. ☐

3 H_w _ wf_l. ☐

4 _'m r _ _ lly s _ rry. ☐

5 _t's _n m_ . ☐

6 H_ , y _ _ l t. ☐

7 _t's n _ t my f _ _ l t. ☐

a I apologise.

b Don't worry.

c What a pity!

d That's terrible.

e Hello, everybody.

f Don't look at me.

g I'll pay for it.

2 Now complete the conversations with some of the phrases in Exercise 1.

CONVERSATION 1

A Hi, Amy. ¹_____ but I can't come tonight.

B ²_____ You'd really enjoy it. It's your kind of music.

A I know. I really want to come but I've got so much work to do for school.

CONVERSATION 2

A ³_____ Are you coming for an ice cream?

B I can't. I haven't got any money.

A What about you two?

C We haven't got any money either.

A Don't worry. ⁴_____ The newsagent gave me ten pounds for catching a shoplifter.

B That's great.

CONVERSATION 3

A I'm sorry I'm late.

B ⁵_____ You're here now. How are things?

A Not good. My mum lost her purse yesterday. We were in a café and she was about to pay for lunch. She looked in her bag and her purse wasn't there.

B Oh, no. ⁶_____

A Mum thinks somebody stole the purse. All her credit cards were in it. She was really upset.

Pronunciation

Short and long vowel sounds: /ɪ/ – /iː/ and /ɒ/ – /əʊ/

Go to page 121. 🔊

Writing part 1

1 In Justin's English class, they have been discussing education. Their teacher has asked them to write an essay for homework: Secondary schools should offer vocational courses – courses that train you for a job.

Read Justin's notes for his essay. Is each point *for* or *against* the idea of vocational courses? Write F (for) or A (against) next to each statement.

1	Students can learn about different careers on vocational courses such as computer technology.	☐
2	On a vocational course, they learn a useful skill that they can use in the future.	☐
3	Students enjoy vocational courses.	☐
4	Vocational courses cost too much money for some schools.	☐
5	They are good for students who find it hard to sit quietly in class.	☐
6	Most parents think getting a degree is better than taking a vocational course.	☐

2 Now read his essay and answer the questions.

1 What do vocational courses prepare students for?

_____

2 Why are parents negative towards vocational courses?

_____

3 What do vocational courses give students the option to do?

_____

3 Read the task and then plan and write your essay.

Some parents choose not to send their children to school. They choose to teach them at home instead. This is called 'home schooling'. The topic for your essay is: Home schooling is a good idea.

Your essay must be 140–190 words.

Include 4 paragraphs:
1 an introduction
2 arguments for
3 arguments against
4 a conclusion

Exam guide: writing an essay

Look back at page 95 to help you write an essay.

- First, think about the statement. Do you agree with it or not?
- Research and plan your argument. List 2 or 3 points *for* and 2 or 3 points *against*.
- Make your opinion clear in the introductory paragraph.
- Remember to use phrases such as: *in my opinion, however*, etc.
- Sum up your argument with a good concluding sentence.

Secondary schools should offer vocational courses

Academic courses prepare students for university but they don't prepare them for a job. Some students want to work when they leave school, and vocational courses prepare them for this. Therefore, I think that we have to include vocational courses in the school curriculum.

Firstly, a vocational course gives students a skill that they can use in everyday life or for work. In addition to getting a skill, students enjoy these courses, and they become more motivated at school. Most importantly, however, they are good for students who find it hard to sit quietly in class.

On the negative side, however, some parents believe that vocational courses encourage students to choose a career such as hairdressing rather than to try for university. Parents believe that a university degree leads to a better job and eventually a higher salary. Furthermore, vocational courses can cost schools a lot of money to provide.

But university isn't for everybody. There are other very interesting careers that don't require a university degree. In my opinion, vocational courses give students the option to discover other jobs and careers that may be more suitable for them.

4 Ask a friend to read your essay and complete the sentences about it.

You have organised / haven't organised your essay

_____

You have used / haven't used phrases such as

_____

You have completed / haven't completed the task

_____

You could improve it by

_____

CONSOLIDATION

LISTENING

1 🔊 **42** **Listen to the dialogue between Rob and Sue. Write in the prices of these items and tick the ones that he bought.**

1 £ _____

2 £ _____

3 £ _____

4 £ _____

2 🔊 **42** **Listen again and mark the sentences T (true) or F (false).**

1 Rob thinks he's missing £18. ☐

2 The CD normally costs £10. ☐

3 Rob stopped at the sweetshop after the bookshop. ☐

4 Sue suggests that someone could have taken his money. ☐

5 Rob asks Sue to buy him a cinema ticket. ☐

6 Matt lends Rob £5. ☐

GRAMMAR

3 (Circle) **the correct options.**

1 You shouldn't *say / have said* that. She's really upset now.

2 She drives a Ferrari. She must *be / have been* rich.

3 This time next week I'll *be lying / have been lying* on a beach in Malta.

4 They'll *be / have been* married for 20 years in December.

5 You spent too much. You should *be / have been* more careful with money.

6 No one passed the test. It can't *be / have been* very easy.

7 If it carries on raining like this, we won't *have played / be playing* tennis at three o'clock.

8 This time next year I will *be studying / have studied* English for four years.

4 **Complete the sentences with two words.**

1 By the time he comes back home, my brother _____ visited twenty countries.

2 This time next week, I'll _____ breakfast in a hotel in Spain.

3 They look very tired. They _____ worked very hard today.

4 You're late! You _____ arrived thirty minutes ago!

5 Someone told me they lost 7–1! They _____ played very well.

VOCABULARY

5 **Match the sentence halves.**

1 The crime remains unexplained, ☐

2 Henry hasn't replied to my email, ☐

3 We're nearly there. ☐

4 Several people reported seeing a mysterious ☐

5 It's not very valuable. It can't be ☐

6 If you're not happy you can bring it ☐

7 My pen's gone missing. ☐

8 You've got to buy it. It's only on ☐

a Only one more kilometre to go.

b back to the shop and get a refund.

c Have you seen it?

d offer for today.

e and to this day, nobody knows what really happened.

f worth more than £50.

g man running from the crime scene.

h which is really puzzling.

6 **Complete each word.**

1 That's o_ _ , I left my sandwich here five minutes ago and now it's gone.

2 I only paid £3 – it was a real b_ _ _ _ _ _ .

3 There's a r_ _ _ _ _ of £20 for the missing cat.

4 I'll tell you but it's a s_ _ _ _ _ and I don't want you to tell anybody.

5 I'm not going to leave the waiter a t _ _ . The service was terrible.

6 Scientists believe the rock is e_ _ _ _ _ _ _ _ _ _ _ _ _ _ and came from another planet.

7 This technology can't be from our planet. It must be a _ _ _ _ .

8 At only £200, it's really good v_ _ _ _ for money.

DIALOGUE

7 Complete the conversation with the phrases in the list. There are two you won't use.

more than likely | you must be joking | a shame | never mind
same as usual | goes without saying | don't look at me | how awful

MARTIN   I don't believe it. Someone's spilt coffee all over my project.

RUTH   ¹_____, I had nothing to do with it.

SOPHIE   It was John, ²_____. He's really clumsy.

MARTIN   Well it ³_____ that I'm not at all happy about it. It's ruined. Look at it.

RUTH   ⁴_____. Can't you do it again?

MARTIN   ⁵_____. It took me three days and it's got to be handed in tomorrow.

SOPHIE   That's ⁶_____. You'll just have to tell the teacher what happened and ask for some more time.

MARTIN   I only hope he'll agree. Just wait until I see John.

READING

8 Read the article and answer the questions.

1 How did the boys find out how the machine worked?

_____

2 Why didn't anyone at the bank believe their story?

_____

3 What evidence did the boys take back to the bank?

_____

4 What else did they do to show they had hacked into the machine?

_____

5 Why did the bank manager write them a note?

_____

WRITING

9 Write a paragraph of about 120 words on your thoughts of money. Include this information.

- how you get money
- what you spend it on
- anything you're saving up for
- ways you could get more money

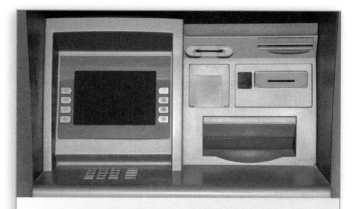

HONEST TEENS IN CASH MACHINE SCANDAL

When Matthew Hewlett and Caleb Turon decided to try and hack into a cash machine they could hardly have imagined how easy it would be. The two 14 year-old Canadians had found a manual explaining how to operate the Bank of Montreal ATM online. In the manual there was a password. One day during their lunch break from school they decided to try out the password at the machine in their local supermarket. To their surprise the six digit password took them straight into the machine's computer where they were able to access all the data it contained.

The boys went straight to the closest branch of the Bank of Montreal where they told workers there what had happened. The bank staff refused to believe the boys, saying that they couldn't have hacked into the machine and that they had no evidence to support their story. So the boys asked if it would be all right if they got some proof. The bank workers agreed that they could but told them they would never be able to get anything out of the cash machine.

The boys returned to the machine and hacked in once again. This time they printed out information such as all the cash withdrawals that had been made that day and how much money was in the machine. They also changed the welcome message on the screen to 'Go away. This machine has been hacked.'

They returned to the bank with the evidence and this time they were taken seriously. The manager of the bank came to thank them personally. He even wrote them a note to show to their teachers explaining why they were so late back from their lunch break!

11 HELP!

GRAMMAR
Verbs followed by gerund or infinitive
SB page 104

1 ★★☆ **Put the words in the correct order to make sentences.**

1 mind / I / you / helping / don't

_____

2 I / buy / can't / it / afford / to

_____

3 promised / tomorrow / to / tell / He / us

_____

4 don't / I / see / them / expect / again / to

_____

5 She / to / café / suggested / the / going

_____

6 favourite / Imagine / film star / meeting / your

_____

2 ★★☆ **Put the verbs in brackets into the correct form, gerund or infinitive.**

There are some lovely hills near where we live, and we enjoy ¹_____ (walk) there at the weekends. But we have learned ²_____ (be) careful and ³_____ (tell) people where we are going. Usually we avoid ⁴_____ (go) up there if the weather is going to be bad.

But one day we decided ⁵_____ (go) up, even though we'd heard it might get foggy. We really wanted ⁶_____ (get) some exercise. So we set off – the weather was nice and sunny, and everything was great. We didn't expect ⁷_____ (have) any problems.

After two hours, we felt like ⁸_____ (have) a rest, so we sat down. And then the fog started coming in. My wife suggested ⁹_____ (go) back immediately, but I wanted ¹⁰_____ (stay) a bit longer. Big mistake! Soon we couldn't see anything – we didn't know which way to go at all. My wife called the emergency services. Twenty minutes later, they found us and helped us back home.

I had never imagined ¹¹_____ (need) to make an emergency phone call. And I have promised myself never ¹²_____ (go) into the hills again when the weather forecast isn't good.

3 ★★★ **Use a verb from each list to complete the sentences in the correct form.**

~~offer~~ | feel like | miss | practise
afford | avoid | promise

~~lend~~ | give | speak | buy
eat | live | study

0 My brother _offered to lend_ me his laptop today so I can do some work.

1 Let's go to the Indian restaurant. I _____ a nice hot curry!

2 Tickets for the concert are really expensive. I can't _____ one.

3 I don't like this city. I really _____ in the country, like we used to.

4 She _____ me her answer tomorrow. I hope she says 'yes'.

5 I love going to France, because then I can _____ French.

6 I always _____ the night before a test.

> ### Pronunciation
> **Strong and weak forms: /tuː/ and /tə/**
> **Go to page 121.** 🔊

to / in order to / so as to SB page 105

4 ★☆☆ Circle the correct words.

We were really happy because we'd got tickets for the big match. We had stood in line for three hours the week before ¹*to / not to* get the tickets.
We got to the stadium early, ²*so as to / so as not to* have to stand in a long queue. On the way we stopped at a shop ³*in order to / in order not to* buy some food and drink – we bought a lot ⁴*so as not to / so as to* feel hungry in the middle of the match.
While we were waiting for the match to begin, the sun came out and we took our pullovers off ⁵*to / to not* get too hot. And then the game began! Unfortunately a couple of really big, tall guys sat in front of us so sometimes we had to stand up ⁶*to / not to* see what was happening. But after two hours, they left, so for the next four hours we had a perfect view of everything. (Oh, didn't I tell you? It was a cricket match – it started at 11 am and finished at 6 pm!)

5 ★★☆ **Make the two sentences into one using the words in brackets.**

0   I got up at 6 am. I wanted to get some good photographs. (in order to)
   I got up at 6 am in order to get some good photographs.

1   We got to the stadium early. We didn't want to miss the start of the game. (so as not to)

2   I phoned Michelle. I wanted to invite her to my party. (to)

3   I didn't tell my parents about the accident. I didn't want to worry them. (so as not to)

4   I took the train. I didn't want to get hot cycling. (in order not to)

5   I'd like to speak to her. I want to apologise. (in order to)

6   He's saving his money. He wants to buy a new computer. (so as to)

so and *such*   SB page 107

6 ★☆☆ **Circle the correct words.**

1   He was *so / such* tired that he just wanted to go to bed.
2   It was *so / such* a difficult question that no one could answer it.
3   It was *so / such* hot that I had to take my jacket off.
4   I ate *so / such* much food yesterday that I was ill.
5   I've lived here *so / such* a long time that I can't even remember our last home.
6   It was *so / such* expensive that I couldn't afford it.

7 ★★☆ **Complete the gaps with *so* or *such a*.**

1   I need to take an aspirin. I've got _____ bad headache.
2   I was _____ scared that I couldn't move.
3   The water was _____ cold that I didn't go in.
4   She's _____ funny girl that we always laugh a lot with her.
5   What he did was _____ brave thing that they gave him a medal.
6   I'm _____ worried about the test tomorrow.

8 ★★★ **Read the sentence pairs. Write a new (third) sentence so that it has the same meaning as the sentence pair. Use *so* and *such*.**

0   I'm really hungry. I'm going to eat another sandwich.
   I'm so hungry that I'm going to eat another sandwich.

1   She's really friendly. I always like being with her.

2   They left very early. They were there before lunch.

3   I've got a bad stomach ache. I might go home.

4   It was a terrible film. We left before the end.

5   The teacher's explanation was complicated. We couldn't understand it.

6   The party was a great success. We're going to have another one next week.

GET IT RIGHT! 👁
Verbs with *to* + base form

With verbs that require *to* + base form, we do not use *for* (+ *to*) + base form.
✓ I went to the cinema **to see** a film.
✗ I went to the cinema ~~for to see~~ a film.

We can use *for* + noun.
✓ I bought some chocolates **for his birthday**
✗ I bought some chocolates ~~for to give~~ him.
✓ I bought some chocolates **to give** him.

Tick the correct sentences. Correct the incorrect ones.

1   I'm here for English lessons. ☐
2   You need to turn on the light for to see better. ☐
3   I use my phone for taking photos. ☐
4   He uses his tablet for to read books. ☐
5   I asked you to give me information. ☐
6   Giraffes have a long neck for to reach the tops of trees. ☐

VOCABULARY

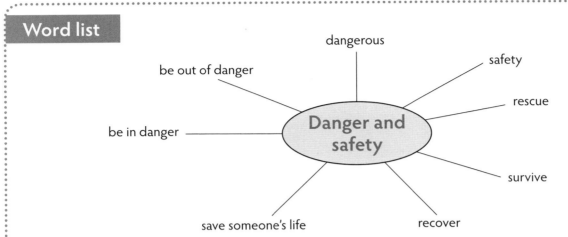

Adjectives with negative prefixes

il-	im-	in-	ir-	un-
illegal illogical	impatient impolite impossible	inexpensive informal	irregular irresponsible	unafraid uncomfortable unconcerned unhappy unhealthy unhelpful unimportant unnecessary unsurprising untrue

Key words in context

bravery	She saved three people's lives, and got a medal for her **bravery**.
buggy	He hadn't learned to walk, so his mother pushed him in a **buggy**.
collapse	Hundreds of houses **collapsed** in the earthquake.
consequence	We got there late, and as a **consequence**, we missed the start of the film.
drill	They used a very big **drill** to make a hole in the ground.
emergency	Please use this door only in an **emergency** (for example, a fire).
miracle	It was a terrible accident – it's a **miracle** that no one was hurt or killed.
tragedy	The pilot prevented a **tragedy** when he landed the plane safely.
trap	They couldn't get out of the house – they were **trapped** inside.
wreck	There is the **wreck** of a ship at the bottom of the sea here.

Danger and safety SB page 104

1 ★★☆ **Complete the sentences.**

1 He was very ill, but now the doctors say that he's o_____ of danger.

2 Thank you so much – you s_____ my life!

3 Don't go in there – it's very d_____ .

4 Two people died in the car crash, but three other people s_____ .

5 The firemen found a man in the burning house and pulled him to s_____ .

6 Their boat sank, but they were r_____ by a passing ship.

7 When we saw the water coming, we knew we were in d_____ , so we ran as fast as we could.

8 After two weeks in hospital, she finally r_____ and was allowed to go home.

2 ★★★ **Use a word or phrase from Exercise 1 in each space.**

I could see that I was in a very ¹_____ situation. I was trying to ²_____ the princess's life, but her enemies were getting very close. Now both of us were ³_____ .

I looked around – how could we escape? There was an open window, but we were on the fifth floor. I looked down – we could jump but I didn't know if we would ⁴_____ the fall. But there were no other options – jumping was the only way that we could get to ⁵_____ .

I turned to the princess. She looked at me. 'Thank you,' she said. 'I've been a prisoner here so long. Thank you for coming to ⁶_____ me.' I smiled. 'No problem, your Highness,' I said. 'But we're not ⁷_____ yet, I'm afraid.'

The princess looked out of the window. 'OK,' she said. 'Let's jump. If we get hurt, there's a chance we'll ⁸_____ before too long.'

I thought: 'How brave she is!' We went to the window. We held hands and …

'Danny!' said my mum. 'Time for dinner. And stop playing that computer game!'

Adjectives with negative prefixes
SB page 107

3 ★☆☆ **Write the negative forms of the words.**

1	happy	_____	6	necessary	_____
2	expensive	_____	7	legal	_____
3	possible	_____	8	formal	_____
4	comfortable	_____	9	patient	_____
5	true	_____	10	polite	_____

4 ★★☆ **Use the words from Exercise 3 to complete the sentences.**

1 She's crying – she must be _____ about something.

2 You don't have to dress smartly – it's an _____ party.

3 Please don't leave without saying goodbye – it's _____ .

4 I'll give you some food in a few minutes – don't be so _____ !

5 No one can pick up 400 kilograms – it's _____ !

6 I didn't sleep well – the bed was very _____ .

7 It's only £5.99 – it's very _____ .

8 They didn't need to have all that violence in the film – it was really _____ .

9 No, I didn't take your rucksack – that's completely _____ !

10 In my country, it is _____ to drive a car if you're under eighteen.

5 ★★★ **Complete the conversation with the words in the list. There are two extra words.**

impolite | saved | illegal | safety | rescued
unnecessary | tragedy | danger | trapped
miracle | unhappy | uncomfortable | recovered
survived

TIM Sue? Look, I really don't want to be ¹_____ , but can you put your seatbelt on please?

SUE But I hate wearing seatbelts, they're very ²_____ . And anyway, I'm in the back seat.

TIM I'm sorry, but you have to. It's the law. It's ³_____ not to wear a seatbelt, even in the back seat.

SUE Well, to be honest, I think if people drive carefully, then seatbelts are ⁴_____ .

TIM I really don't agree. A friend of mine was in an accident and her seatbelt ⁵_____ her life. She was a passenger in the back seat of a car that crashed. It's a ⁶_____ that she ⁷_____ .

SUE Really?

TIM Yes, her leg was ⁸_____ . She was in the car for almost an hour, but the fire service ⁹_____ her.

SUE Wow.

TIM They took her to hospital. Her life was in ¹⁰_____ for almost 24 hours. But she ¹¹_____ OK, I'm happy to say. It was almost a ¹²_____ , though.

SUE OK, you've convinced me. I'm going to wear a seatbelt from now on!

READING

1 **REMEMBER AND CHECK** There is one mistake in each sentence. <u>Underline</u> it and write the correct word(s). Then check your answers in the article on page 103 of the Student's Book.

0 George Reeder is a <u>postmaster</u> in Watchet, Somerset.   *harbour master*

1 When he heard a noise, he ran over to see what was happening.   _____

2 He saw a baby in about four metres of warm water.   _____

3 The baby spent three minutes in the sea.   _____

4 There was a passer-by who was a doctor.   _____

5 The baby was taken to hospital by boat.   _____

6 The baby's father came to Mr Reeder's house to say he was out of danger.   _____

7 Mr Reeder was given a medal for his bravery.   _____

2 Look at the numbers 1–6. What do you think they refer to? Match to the letters a–f. Then read the book review and check.

1	1,000+	a	the number of penguins covered by the oil
2	75,000	b	the number of tons of fish needed every day to feed the penguins
3	20,000	c	the number of tons of oil that went into the sea
4	12	d	the number of weeks that were needed to save the penguins
5	45,000	e	the number of penguins that lived in the area
6	10	f	the number of people who helped to save the penguins

3 Read the review again. Answer the questions.

1 What was the problem for the penguins covered in oil?

_____

2 Why did the rescue operation work?

_____

3 Where did they take the penguins?

_____

4 What were the two problems with feeding the penguins?

_____

5 How did they remove the oil from the penguins?

_____

6 Why did the penguins have to be put into pools?

_____

7 What was special about this rescue?

_____

8 What can you find out at the end of the book?

_____

The Great Penguin Rescue
by Dyan deNapoli

This great book is a true story. On June 23, 2000 a ship called *MV Treasure* sank near Cape Town, South Africa. More than a thousand tons of oil went into the ocean, near an area where 75,000 penguins lived. Roughly 20,000 African penguins were covered with oil and as a result couldn't swim or even walk properly. It was very possible that they would die. A huge rescue operation was begun, and it lasted for twelve weeks. The operation was only successful because 45,000 people offered to give their time and energy, for free, to the project.

The rescue was a success, but it wasn't easy at any stage. First, the penguins were caught and taken to a special recovery centre. When they got there, the penguins were kept in a quiet place for several days so that they got used to their new 'home'. During this time, and throughout the three months, the penguins had to be fed. It isn't easy to find enough fish to feed 20,000 penguins (about ten tons a day), and feeding penguins isn't easy either: they have extremely sharp beaks and many volunteers

got wounds on their arms from penguin bites.

After that, the oil had to be removed from the penguins' feathers. Each penguin was washed in detergent, and then it was put under a heating lamp to dry. This was done again and again until there was no more oil on the penguin. The penguins then had to be put in pools to swim every day until their feathers recovered completely. 'The Great Penguin Rescue' was the world's biggest rescue of live animals. It's a moving story because so many people took part in the rescue and showed that they really cared about saving an endangered species.

This is a wonderful book, and right at the end the author even tells you how to go about adopting a penguin.

DEVELOPING WRITING

A rescue story

1 Read the story. What did the divers think the whale did after she was freed?

Sometimes, it's amazing when an animal is involved in a rescue.

Back in 2005, some fishermen were working at sea near San Francisco when they saw a whale that was in ¹_____ trouble. The ²_____ humpback whale was caught in some ropes and she could not swim properly. The ropes also had heavy weights on them that were making it difficult for the whale to come up to breathe.

Some divers realised that the only way that they could save the whale was to go into the water and try to cut the ropes. This was ³_____ dangerous, since one hit from the whale's ⁴_____ tail could kill them. But the men jumped in. They were worried that they wouldn't be able to save it. The rope was so tight around the whale that it was cutting her body. She was dying.

The divers worked for an ⁵_____ hour cutting away the ropes. ⁶_____ the whale was free and started swimming again.

And then an amazing thing happened. The whale began to swim in circles, coming up to each of the divers and pushing her nose into them. She seemed to be thanking them and even though it was huge they didn't feel ⁷_____ threatened.

Experts on whales say it's hard to imagine that the whale was really saying 'Thank you'. But the divers don't care. They all agreed that it was an ⁸_____ experience.

2 Complete the article with the words in the list. There is sometimes more than one possibility.

enormous | eventually | exhausting | huge
incredibly | remotely | terrible | unbelievable

3 Use a word from Exercise 2 to replace the <u>underlined</u> words in these sentences.

1 It was a <u>big</u> problem. _____
2 We had to walk for two hours – it was <u>hard</u>! _____
3 The film was <u>very</u> exciting. _____
4 It was a <u>bad</u> moment. _____
5 <u>In the end</u> we got home. _____
6 I wasn't <u>even a little bit</u> scared. _____

4 Write a story about a rescue. Choose one of the following sentences to begin your story.

A Sometimes it's amazing when an animal is involved in a rescue.
B It was a bad mistake to go there in the first place.
C 'Lucky to be alive' was never truer than in this story.

Write between 200 and 250 words.

Writing tip: a story

- Think about the content of your story (it can be real or invented).
- Think about how to make it as interesting and dramatic as you can for the reader.
- Look again at the Exam guide in Unit 4 to help you.
- Use extreme adjectives and verbs to make your story exciting.
- Think about your sentences. Short sentences can make your story more dramatic.

CHECKLIST ✔

☐ Beginning, middle and end
☐ Use interesting adjectives and adverbs
☐ Use long and short sentences

LISTENING

1 🔊44 **Listen to two conversations. Mark the sentences T (true) or F (false) or NG (the information is not given).**

CONVERSATION 1

1 Jordan is wearing trainers with holes in them. ☐

2 He does many things to annoy his mum. ☐

3 He thinks his clothes are comfortable. ☐

4 Jordan chooses his clothes so as to be different to other people his age. ☐

CONVERSATION 2

5 Janet is the best young cyclist in the country. ☐

6 Janet thinks you need to train and have talent to be a top cyclist. ☐

7 Janet never goes out alone to train. ☐

8 Janet believes that cycling is a team sport. ☐

2 🔊44 **Listen again. Complete these parts of the conversations.**

A

MUM   Why do you dress like this, Jordan?

JORDAN   Well, Mum, I promise, it isn't
   1_____ you.

MUM   Really?

JORDAN   Really! I dress like this because I like it. And 2_____ comfortable.

MUM   Oh, comfortable!

JORDAN   Yes, Mum. And it's 3_____ different, too.

B

LARRY   What does it take 4_____ to the top in a sport like cycling?

JANET   Hard work, Larry! Cycling's not easy and you have to work hard, train a lot, 5_____ in the best physical condition possible.

LARRY   And you need talent, too, I guess.

JANET   Well, yes. You know, 6_____ a top cyclist, you have to love cycling and have a certain talent for it.

DIALOGUE

1 **Put the dialogues in order.**

1

☐ A Oh? Why not?

[1] A Where are you going?

☐ A Why on earth do you want a new one?

☐ A To get some things?

☐ B Into town.

☐ B To have the same one as everyone else, of course.

☐ B So as not to spend any money. I'm saving up for a new phone.

☐ B No, just window shopping today. I'm not going to buy anything.

2

☐ A A marathon? What on earth for?

☐ A Why's that?

[1] A Wow, that's not much food. Not hungry?

☐ A Fitter? Are you going to start running or something?

☐ B No, I've just decided I want to eat less.

☐ B To lose weight, to look better, and to get fitter.

☐ B So as to get money for charity.

☐ B Actually, I've already started. I go to the gym too. It's in order to run a marathon.

2 **Write two dialogues of four to six lines each.**

For each one:

● choose a person from the list below;

● think of 'why' questions to ask the person;

● think of the person's answer(s).

Look back at Exercise 1 to help you.

Someone who wrote a book review

Someone who jumped into a freezing cold river

Someone who wants to be a firefighter

Someone who wants to work for a charity organisation

_____

_____

_____

_____

_____

_____

_____

_____

_____

_____

Reading and Use of English part 6

Exam guide: gapped text

You will read a text from which six sentences have been removed. Your task is to say where these sentences fit into the text. There is one extra sentence that doesn't belong anywhere.

- Read through the text to get a good understanding of what it is about.
- Look carefully at each space. Read the whole paragraph carefully. Then concentrate on the sentences immediately before and after. What information do you think might be missing to connect the sentences?
- Now look at the options. Do any of them contain the information that's needed?

- Look carefully at any reference words in the options. Use them to help you make connections between the sentences.
- Connecting words can sometimes help you see the links between the sentences.
- Leave any gap that you find difficult and come back to it later. If you still don't know the answer, then guess.

1 You are going to read a text about a boy who had a scary experience while on holiday. Six sentences have been removed from the text. Choose from the sentences A–G the one that fits each gap (1–6). There is one extra sentence which you do not need to use.

Trapped!

Last year I went on holiday to the French Alps with my parents and brother. We are all keen mountain climbers and we were looking forward to five days of climbing. We weren't planning to get to any great height but rather concentrate on a series of challenging smaller climbs.

The first day we tackled a 50 metre cliff face. It was a popular climb and there were several teams doing the same thing. It wasn't too difficult and we were all at the top within a couple of hours. (1) ☐ It was about 11 am and the sun was really starting to warm the rock face. We didn't fancy making the descent in the midday sun so we decided to wait a few hours and explore the surroundings. My brother and I went off to explore some nearby caves. We'd done a bit of caving before and these caves looked pretty exciting. They were deep and dark. After about 10 metres the passageway became really narrow. I told my brother we'd better leave. (2) ☐ He could hear water and was sure there was an underground lake not far ahead. I wasn't so sure but before I knew it my brother had squeezed through the passage. (3) ☐ Reluctantly I started pushing myself through the narrow gap. I was scared. It was pitch black and I couldn't see a thing. I felt the cold rock pushing against my chest. I was finding it hard to breathe. And then suddenly I was stuck. (4) ☐ I couldn't

move forwards and I couldn't move backwards. I screamed out to my brother. He could just reach my arm. He pulled and pulled but it was no good. I was going nowhere. Of course, he couldn't go and get help because I was blocking his way out.

For ten minutes we yelled and yelled but no one came. My body was sore and although the walls of the cave were cold, a hot sweat covered my body. I was beginning to feel dizzy. (5) ☐ I was sure we were going to die there.

After what felt like hours we heard voices calling our names. I was too weak to respond but my brother called back. Within seconds our parents were with us. My dad tried pulling me out. I screamed out in pain and he realised that we needed professional help.

The helicopter arrived more than two hours later. My body was freezing. (6) ☐ I was barely conscious when the rescue team arrived. They knew exactly what to do. They sprayed a substance over the rock face and then slowly started to pull gently. Then with one sudden jerk I was free. I'd never felt so happy. Then amazingly a few seconds later I was joined by my brother who just squeezed himself back through with no problem at all.

I was taken by helicopter to hospital but released that evening. Apart from a bit of bruising I was fine.

A My parents later told me they were scared they were going to lose me.

B He wanted to continue.

C My leg was broken in two places.

D I wriggled and wriggled but it was no good.

E My brother kept talking to me to keep me conscious.

F He called me to join him.

G The views were incredible.

12 | A FIRST TIME FOR EVERYTHING

GRAMMAR

Phrasal verbs SB page 112

1 ★☆☆ **Complete the sentences with one word. Some of the verbs are from Unit 7.**

0 Why don't you come ___*round*___ to my place this evening?

1 I didn't have anything to do, so I ended _____ going to bed!

2 Let's go online and find _____ what time the film starts.

3 It was a difficult question so in the end I looked _____ the answer online.

4 He's much taller than the rest of our family, so he really stands _____ in photos.

5 From our back garden, you can see planes taking _____ from the airport.

6 Last night I hung _____ with my friends in the park.

2 ★★☆ (Circle) **the correct phrasal verb and write it in the correct form.**

0 She __*blew out*__ the candles on her birthday cake. ((blow out)/ stand out)

1 We're really _____ the summer holidays. (look after / look forward to)

2 I haven't found the answer yet, but I'm going to _____ looking for it! (carry on / carry out)

3 I'm sorry, I can't come tonight. I've got some things to _____ at home. (hang out / sort out)

4 We left early, but then our car _____ so we arrived very late. (set off / break down)

5 Paula was really late – she only _____ at 10 o'clock. (end up / show up)

6 We didn't like the new neighbours at first, but now we _____ well with them. (get on / end up)

7 My dad has _____ the piano. His first lesson was last Monday. (take up / take off)

8 My friends are going to _____ to my house after school. (come round / come up)

3 ★★☆ (Circle) **the correct options.**

1 There's a concert tonight. I'm really *looking forward to it / looking forward it to*.

2 Oh, so you're learning the guitar? When did you *take up it / take it up*?

3 We had an argument, but we *sorted it out / sorted out it* and now we get on well again.

4 We made a small fire for our barbecue – but the wind *blew out it / blew it out*!

5 My sister's not well, but my mum's *looking her after / looking after her*.

6 We were going to fly there, but when we *worked it out / worked out it*, the train was cheaper.

7 They have started some new research and they will *carry it out / carry out it* over the next year.

4 ★★★ **Complete the diary entry with a phrasal verb from the list in the correct form and, where necessary, a pronoun (*it / them / him / her* etc.).**

carry out | look forward to | look after
end up | get on | carry on
break down | come round | hang out

April 1st

Today is April Fool's Day! I always have lots of ideas for jokes to play on people, but I never ⁰ *carry them out*. I thought about playing an April Fool's joke on my friend Steve but I didn't, because I didn't want to ¹_____ losing him as a friend – Steve and I ²_____ well together so I don't want to change that with a silly joke. I want to ³_____ being friends with him. When we go on holiday I give my pet snake to Steve and he ⁴_____.

And yes – holidays! In a few weeks we've got a one-week holiday at school. I'm really ⁵_____, because my dad says we can go to the beach. So that's nice. What isn't nice is that Dad wants to go in his car and his car always ⁶_____ if we go more than ten kilometres. I don't know why he doesn't get a new one.

Tonight I'm going to ⁷_____ with Alex and Sam at the shopping centre. I wanted them to ⁸_____ to my house but they said 'No thanks'. I wonder why?

I wish / If only + past perfect `SB page 115`

5 ★★☆ (Circle) the correct options.

Andy went to a party and he really wanted to dance with Sarah. But it didn't go well. Here's what he thinks.

1 'I wish I *hadn't gone / didn't go* to the party.'

2 'I wish Paul *hadn't invited / didn't invite* me.'

3 'If only *I knew / I'd known* about the terrible music.'

4 'I wish *I took / I'd taken* some of my favourite music.'

5 'If only *they'd played / they played* that Katy Perry song – Sarah would have danced with me.'

6 'If only Sarah *had danced / danced* with me! But Mike was there.'

7 'I wish Mike *wasn't / hadn't been* there.'

8 'And I wish I *hadn't worn / didn't wear* my pink trousers.'

6 ★★☆ Read what Sarah says and write sentences using *I wish* or *If only*.

0 'Andy didn't ask me to dance.'
  I wish Andy had asked me to dance.

1 'Andy wore pink trousers.'
  _____

2 'They played terrible music.'
  _____

3 'Mike wasn't in a good mood.'
  _____

4 'Andy ate so much food.'
  _____

5 'Mike laughed at Andy.'
  _____

6 'Andy didn't enjoy himself.'
  _____

7 'My parents took me home at midnight.'
  _____

8 'I didn't have a good time.'

7 ★★★ Look at the pictures. For each person, write a sentence using *I wish / if only*.

1 _____   2 _____
  _____   _____

3 _____   4 _____
  _____   _____

GET IT RIGHT! 👁

Separable verbs

Learners often have problems with word order when using separable verbs.

✓ A car **ran them over**.

✗ A car ~~ran over them~~.

Choose the correct sentence from the pairs. Sometimes both sentences are correct.

1 a I will pick you up at 7.30.
  b I will pick up you at 7.30.

2 a When I left, I forgot to take out my memory stick.
  b When I left, I forgot to take my memory stick out.

3 a I looked for a telephone number in my phone.
  b I looked a telephone number for in my phone.

4 a I would like to get back my money for that trip.
  b I would like to get my money back for that trip.

5 a You should think over it.
  b You should think it over.

6 a The man gave me my bag back.
  b The man gave me back my bag.

VOCABULARY

Phrasal verbs (2)

blow out	There were fifteen candles on my birthday cake, but I **blew** them **out** in one go.
break down	We were late because our car **broke down** and we missed the beginning of the play.
carry out	Scientists **carry out** experiments to understand things better.
look forward to	Our holiday is going to be great! I'm really **looking forward to** it.
look into	The police are **looking into** the crime and hope to find out who did it.
sort out	I had a problem with my phone but my sister **sorted** it **out**.
stand out	White writing on blue paper really **stands out**.
work out	I can't **work out** why she's angry with me. What did I do?

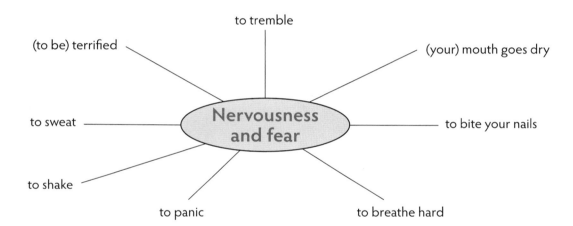

Key words in context

bungee jumping	I went **bungee jumping** in Australia – it was exciting but scary!
candle	All the lights went out in our house, so we had to use **candles** to see.
childhood	She had a very happy **childhood**, growing up in Scotland.
innovation	This year there were lots of **innovations** in mobile phone technology.
item	He went to a store and bought seven **items** of clothing.
powerful	This car's got a very **powerful** engine, so it goes very fast.
roughly	**Roughly** 70 million people live in Britain.
stumble (through)	I made lots of mistakes in my speech but I managed to **stumble through** to the end.

Phrasal verbs (2) `SB page 112`

1 ★★☆ **Complete the sentences with the correct preposition.**

1 The wind blew _____ all the candles.

2 On the way to school the bus broke _____ and we had to walk.

3 Someone stole a bike at school yesterday. The headmaster is looking _____ it.

4 I'm looking forward _____ seeing my cousin again.

5 Some scientists are carrying _____ research about that illness.

6 My mum's not here – she has to sort _____ a problem at work.

7 They look so like each other – I can never work _____ who is who!

8 I want to be like everyone else – I don't want to stand _____ !

9 I can't come out tonight, I'm looking _____ my younger brother.

10 You carry _____ going, I'll meet you there.

2 ★★☆ **Complete the phrasal verbs with one word in the correct form.**

1

A How was your trip? I know you were really ¹_____ forward to it.

B Er – well, it wasn't very good.

A Oh? What happened?

B Well, the car ²_____ down. At night! Dad looked at the engine but he couldn't ³_____ out what was wrong. We had to get a truck to take it to the garage. They ⁴_____ the car out there, and we were able to continue our trip.

2

A So, was the party good?

B Not really. No one told me it was fancy dress – I was the only person in normal clothes, so I really ⁵_____ out. And there were one or two people with masks on their faces, so I couldn't ⁶_____ out who they were.

3

A How's your brother's new job?

B Great! He loves it. He's ⁷_____ out some research for a professor at the university. The professor is ⁸_____ into ways of making water clean in poor countries.

A Sounds really interesting.

Nervousness and fear `SB page 115`

3 ★★☆ **Complete the crossword.**

1 Some people do this if they are very hot or very nervous.

2 Even if you are frightened, you should try not to do this.

3 Sometimes people bite these when they are nervous.

4 Some people do this if they are very cold or very nervous.

5 Very, very scared.

6 Some people do this hard when they are tired or afraid.

7 Some people do this when they are afraid or nervous.

8 Sometimes this goes dry if you are nervous.

4 ★★★ **Complete the words in the story in the correct form.**

When I arrived for my interview, I was a bit nervous. They showed me to a waiting room – there were three other people there. One man looked terrible – he was ¹b_____ his n_____ and walking up and down the room. He was walking slowly, but even so, he was ²b_____ h_____ . The woman was ³s_____ a lot and she had to keep wiping her face. And the other guy looked very scared, ⁴t_____ in fact! He was ⁵t_____ all the time, and talking to himself very quietly.

I sat down and tried to relax but it wasn't easy with those people around me. I looked at my hands – they were ⁶s_____ a bit, so I took some deep breaths to calm down. 'Don't ⁷p_____ !' I said to myself. 'It'll be OK.'

When I finally went in and they asked me a question, my ⁸m_____ went completely d_____ and I could hardly speak. I thought the interview had gone really badly. But in the end I got the job!

READING

1 `REMEMBER AND CHECK` **Complete the summary of the text with the words in the list. Then check your answers in the article on page 111 of the Student's Book.**

research | crystallise | childhood | more often | the near future | before | work out | memories

Many adults don't remember a lot about their early ¹_____ . Scientists have done ²_____ to show that we form ³_____ when we're young, but the way it happens changes as we get older.

The scientists asked 140 children some questions, and then they asked them the same questions again two years later. Younger children said something very different the second time, but older children (between 10 and 13) gave the same answers as ⁴_____ . So it seems that when we are about ten years old, our memories ⁵_____ .

We remember good things ⁶_____ than bad things. Researchers are trying to ⁷_____ why that's the case, and we're going to know more about this in ⁸_____ .

2 **Read the article. Find something that Jackie Robinson and Oprah Winfrey have in common, and something that they don't have in common.**

African-American firsts

In 2008, Barack Obama became the first African-American president of the United States. This was another victory in a long history of firsts for African-American people in the USA. Here are two more that perhaps you don't know about.

1 Jackie Robinson: the first African-American player in Major League Baseball (MLB)

Jackie Robinson

In 1947, Jackie Robinson ran onto the field to play for the Brooklyn Dodgers in New York. Some of the players on the other team, and even some players in his own team, weren't happy to play with him.

But more and more African-American fans started to go to Dodgers' games, and Robinson played exceptionally well. He became more and more famous, even though he had to suffer abuse for many years from many people – players, coaches and fans.

Jackie Robinson was chosen as the best player in the MLB in 1949 and then, in 1962, he became a member of the Baseball Hall of Fame – of course, the first African-American to do so. He was also the first black vice-president of a major American company. He died in 1972, aged 53.

Robinson always wore the number 42, and in 1992, the MLB announced that no other player would ever wear that number. Several films have been made about his life, including the film *42*, made in 2013.

2 Oprah Winfrey: the first African-American woman to host a TV show in the USA

Oprah Winfrey

In 1986, Oprah Winfrey became the first African-American woman to host a TV show in the USA – the *Oprah Winfrey Show*. Her 'book-of-the-month' feature on the show often takes books that are almost unknown and turns them into bestsellers.

Winfrey is one of the highest-paid celebrities in the world. She appeared in the film *The Color Purple* in 1985, and in the film of Toni Morrison's *Beloved* (1998). In April 2000 she launched *O* magazine, which became one of the most successful magazines in publishing history. In April 2002, Winfrey launched the first international edition of *O* in South Africa. In 2003, *Forbes* magazine listed her as the first African-American woman to be a billionaire.

Several times, *Time* magazine has included Oprah in their list of the 100 Most Influential People in the World. She works hard to promote education for women and for African-American children. She has also run high-profile campaigns: for example, to encourage people not to write text messages while they're driving.

3 **Read the article again. Mark the sentences T (true), F (false) or DS (the text doesn't say).**

1 Barack Obama was the first African-American to try to become President of the USA. ☐

2 Only players in other teams didn't want to play with Jackie Robinson. ☐

3 Many people said bad things about Robinson. ☐

4 No African-American has ever been president of a US company. ☐

5 Some baseball players in the MLB still wear the number 42. ☐

6 Oprah Winfrey is a TV presenter and an actress. ☐

7 Winfrey is the first African-American to be a billionaire. ☐

8 She works as a teacher for African-American women and children. ☐

Pronunciation

Different pronunciations of *ea*
Go to page 121. 🔊

DEVELOPING WRITING

A blog entry about a mistake

1 Read the blog entry. What was the effect of the writer's mistake?

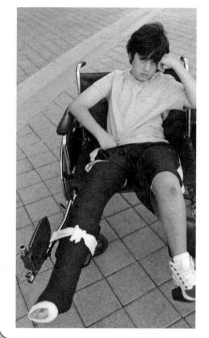

A big mistake

If only I'd stopped to think! That's what I say when I look back at that big mistake. I was 12 and I'd started to play tennis. I couldn't get enough of it. When there was no one to play with, I used to hit tennis balls against a wall. And the best wall was at my school, not far from my house. It was about six metres high. Perfect!

There was a hole in the fence around the school so sometimes I crawled through it, into the school yard to hit tennis balls against that wall. I wasn't supposed to be there after school hours, but I didn't care.

One evening I was there hitting my only tennis ball when it went up onto the roof, rolled down, and into the gutter. Stuck. Now what was I going to do? I had to get it down again. I had to! There was a drainpipe on the wall, going up to the gutter – I didn't think, I just started to climb. I got to the top, and started to go carefully along the gutter. Was I crazy? Absolutely! And what happened? The gutter broke, of course, and I fell.

I could have been killed. Luckily someone had seen what happened and called an ambulance. I'd broken my right leg. The doctors did their best but it never mended properly. My parents were angry because I'd done such a dangerous thing. The school was angry because I shouldn't have been there. I was unhappy because I was in hospital.

If only I'd stopped to think! But I was only 12, after all.

2 Find three 'questions' that the writer asks.

1 Are they really questions for the reader?

2 What effect does the writer want to create by using them?

3 Find three times that the writer uses a single word as a sentence. What effect does the writer want to create by doing this? (Circle) the answer.

A avoid problems with grammar

B create more impact

C use fewer words

4 Rewrite the <u>underlined</u> parts. Use either a question or a single word.

1 I told him the news. <u>This was a mistake</u>!

2 He got really angry and started shouting. <u>I didn't know why he was shouting at me</u>.

3 There clearly was a problem. <u>I didn't know what it was</u>.

4 Then he walked out and closed the door. <u>He closed it loudly</u>.

5 Write a blog entry about a mistake that you (or someone you know) once made. It can be true or invented. Start or finish with one of these sentences.

I wish I hadn't said it.

If only I'd known that I was breaking the rules.

I wish he / she / they had told me.

If only I hadn't opened that door.

I wish I / he / she / they had gone straight home.

Write about 250 words

CHECKLIST ✔

- Opening sentence
- 'I wish' or 'If only' sentences
- Include questions for dramatic effect
- Include one-word 'sentences' for dramatic effect
- Write a suitable ending

LISTENING

1 [◀))46] **Listen to two conversations. Answer the questions.**

CONVERSATION 1

1 What does Jamie regret?

_____

CONVERSATION 2

2 Why is Dave unhappy with Clare?

_____

2 [◀))46] **Listen again. Answer the questions.**

CONVERSATION 1

1 How much did Jamie pay?

_____

2 Why does Anna know so much about buying the tablet online?

_____

3 What does Anna regret at the end?

_____

CONVERSATION 2

4 What is the secret that Clare tells Dave?

_____

5 Why does Clare think it's OK to tell him the secret?

_____

6 Why is it a problem that Clare has told Sam the secret?

_____

3 **Complete the lines from the conversations with the verbs in the list in the correct form.**

do | say | keep | know | tell (x2)

1
JAMIE No, I didn't know that. But I wish
_____ last week!

2
JAMIE If only I _____ a bit of research.
I'm such a fool

3
ANNA Now I wish I _____ you about it!

4
CLARE Did you know his dad had been in prison?
DAVE No, I didn't, and I wish you _____
me.

5
CLARE Well, I wish you _____ something.

6
DAVE Sam can't keep a secret and you know it.
Oh, if only you _____ quiet!

DIALOGUE

1 **Put the lines in order to make three short dialogues.**

DIALOGUE 1
PAUL Oh Vicky, if only you'd been on time.
VICKY _____
PAUL _____
VICKY _____
PAUL _____

DIALOGUE 2
MIKE I wish we hadn't come to this restaurant.
FRANCES _____
MIKE _____
FRANCES _____
MIKE _____

DIALOGUE 3
MANDY My parents are furious with me.
SEAN _____
MANDY _____
SEAN _____
MANDY _____

1 And it's such a shame. The show was amazing.
2 What? Bad reviews? If only you'd told me that before. We could have gone somewhere else.
3 I know. But it wasn't my fault. It was the traffic.
4 I know! If only I'd left when Jim and Sally did – then I wouldn't be in all this trouble.
5 Yes, exactly. I wish I hadn't gone to that party. I didn't even enjoy it.
6 But we came here because you said you wanted to eat Indian food.
7 I wish I had left earlier. But that's history. I missed the show.
8 I'm not surprised. I found lots of bad reviews online about the food here.
9 Well, if you didn't enjoy it, why didn't you leave earlier? You're crazy.
10 There's always traffic. Why didn't you leave home earlier?
11 Why's that? Is it because you were out late on Saturday?
12 I know, and usually I love Indian food, but this isn't good at all.

2 **Choose one of the lines below and use it to start or end a five line dialogue.**

I wish I hadn't come.

I wish I'd never bought it.

If only I hadn't eaten so much.

If only I'd checked on the Internet.

Reading and Use of English part 6

1 You are going to read another extract from *Bullring Kid and Country Cowboy*. Six sentences have been removed from the text. Choose from the sentences A–G the one that fits each gap (1–6). There is one extra sentence that you do not need to use.

Look back at the guide on page 107 in Unit 11 to help you.

Fletcher and Fizza climbed quietly down the hill a few more metres and looked out carefully from behind a small bush. Cloudy's kidnapper was talking to another man who he had met on the beach. (1) ☐ In the dark they could see that one of them was fat and the other one was thin. It was the thin one that had stolen Cloudy.

'Well done! That looks like a nice horse!' the fat man said.

'Yes, we should get a good price for it,' replied the thin man. 'When's the boat going to get here?'

'Any moment now ... I'll get the others,' said the fat man.

He disappeared behind some big rocks in a corner of the beach. After a few seconds he came back out of the dark. (2) ☐

'They're our horses!' whispered Fletcher angrily. 'Those men have been keeping them here!'

The men were obviously waiting for a boat that would get them off the island. A few moments later a green light flashed three times out at sea.

'Hey! That's the sign! They're here!' the thin man shouted.

Fizza and Fletcher realised that if they were going to stop these men, they had to act now before help arrived.

'OK, Fizza,' whispered Fletcher, 'this is what we've got to do ...'

Seconds later Fizza waited in her position while Fletcher gave a low whistle. All three horses on the sand put their heads up and listened, but the men didn't notice anything. (3) ☐ Then Fletcher whistled again and the horses began to jump in excitement. This *did* surprise the men. Every time Fletcher whistled, the horses jumped until they had managed to pull their ropes free from the men's hands. They began to run in circles around them.

'Catch them, stupid!' shouted one of the men.

'You try! They're too quick!' replied the other one.

(4) ☐ She ran onto the beach, jumped in the air, gave a high kick and knocked the fat man down to the ground.

'Oi!' shouted the thin man. He tried to run and help his friend, but all three horses moved into his way.

(5) ☐ Fizza sat on top of the fat man, who lay face down, and held his arms behind his back.

'Ow! That hurts!' he cried.

'Well, don't move then!' replied Fizza.

She watched as Fletcher tied the thin man's hands and feet together with a rope and then she looked out to sea. (6) ☐ 'What are we going to do when that boat gets here?' she asked Fletcher.

'Yeah!' said the fat man through a mouthful of sand. 'What *are* you going to do?'

A	He was leading two large horses.		E	The lights from the kidnappers' boat were getting much nearer, making the horses run away.
B	He couldn't move!		F	The men were so close that Fizza and Fletcher could hear them speak.
C	They were too busy looking for their boat.			
D	He had three other men with him.		G	This was the moment Fizza was waiting for.

CONSOLIDATION

LISTENING

1 ◀)47 **Listen to Billy talking about the first time he went surfing and answer the questions.**

1   How old was he?

   _____

2   How long was he in the water for before he went out to the big waves?

   _____

3   What did he do when he realised he was alone in the water?

   _____

4   Who rescued him?

   _____

2 ◀)47 **Complete the sentences about Billy with the words in the list. Then listen again and check.**

confident | embarrassed | excited
relieved | scared | worried

Billy felt …

1   _____ when his cousins offered to take him surfing.

2   _____ after half an hour in the shallow water.

3   _____ after a few minutes in the deep water.

4   _____ after the big wave had taken his surfboard from him.

5   _____ when he saw the life guard approaching.

6   _____ when he was lying on the beach.

VOCABULARY

3 **Complete the second sentences with negative prefixes.**

1   It's not possible.
   It's _____ .

2   He's not very patient.
   He's quite _____ .

3   The party's not formal.
   It's an _____ .

4   I expect you to be more responsible.
   I don't expect you to be so _____ .

5   This sofa's not very comfortable.
   It's a very _____ .

6   I'm not sure what you're doing is legal.
   I think what you're doing _____ .

4 **Match the sentence halves.**

1   The doctors did everything they could to save ☐

2   He's still in hospital but doctors say he's out ☐

3   That house is very old. It's in ☐

4   When I get nervous I can't stop ☐

5   Does your mouth go ☐

6   Sorry we're late but our car broke ☐

7   I'm really looking ☐

8   I've just got to sort ☐

9   With his blue and red hair, Josh certainly stands ☐

a   danger of falling down.

b   down and we had to wait for a mechanic.

c   forward to the summer holidays.

d   out this problem then I'll help you.

e   of danger now.

f   out from the other boys at his school.

g   dry when you're scared?

h   his life after the accident.

i   biting my nails.

GRAMMAR

5 **Use the verb in brackets to complete the sentences.**

1   I haven't got any money for the bus. I wish I _____ all my money. (not spend)

2   I don't really enjoy _____ . I just do it for exercise. (swim)

3   Dad offered _____ us a lift to the party. (give)

4   They've just bought a new car so they can't afford _____ on holiday this year. (go)

5   If I only I _____ more for breakfast. I'm really hungry. (eat)

6   We moved to the city last year and I really miss _____ in the countryside. (live)

7   I don't mind _____ you. I'm not busy. (help)

8   I wish I _____ my homework last night. There's no time to do it now. (do)

9   I'm really looking forward to _____ my old friends tomorrow. (see)

DIALOGUE

6 Put the dialogue in order.

	ASSISTANT	No, no, don't tell me. And keep the keypad covered up with your other hand.
	ASSISTANT	Here, let me help you. Put the card in like this and now enter your password.
	ASSISTANT	You've got your card in the wrong way.
1	ASSISTANT	Is this your first time using the cash machine?
	ASSISTANT	Well, that's what I'm here for, in order to help our customers.
	ASSISTANT	So as to keep it secret. You don't want other people seeing your password.
	OLD MAN	OK, five, four …
	OLD MAN	That's so embarrassing.
	OLD MAN	Of course I don't. You're such a kind young lady to help me.
	OLD MAN	Yes, it is. How did you guess?
	OLD MAN	Why do I need to do that?
	OLD MAN	In that case, could you help me with my shopping at the supermarket, too?

READING

7 Read the article and mark the sentences T (true) or F (false).

Barnet fans strike it lucky

Edgar Davids made a name for himself playing for some of Europe's greatest football teams such as Milan, Juventus, Ajax and Barcelona as well as being a regular for the Dutch international team during the 1990s and 2000s. Fans of the relatively unknown London club Barnet could hardly believe their luck when he announced his first job as a coach would be with their team, especially when they heard that he was also going to play for them and do all this for free.

But for one group of fans, his move to the team proved to be even luckier. The fans had been to see their team playing against Accrington Stanley in the north of the country. They were half way through the long journey back to London when their bus broke down leaving them stranded by the side of the motorway.

A while later, Davids and the Barnet players were travelling down the same road when Davids noticed the fans freezing by the side of the road. He told the bus driver to stop at the next motorway service station. He then told the players to get off the bus and get something to eat while he sent the bus back to rescue the unfortunate fans. The bus picked up the fans, who were only too happy to get out of the cold just as it started to rain hard. They were then taken to the service station where they met Davids and the players, who were happy to chat, sign autographs and pose for photos. After a while, Davids and his team said goodbye and got back on their bus to continue their journey. The fans were now able to wait in the warmth for their replacement bus, which arrived soon after to take them back home.

1 Barnet are a big English football club.
2 Edgar Davids earned a small salary at Barnet.
3 Davids felt sorry for the fans at the side of the road.
4 Davids went back on the bus to get the fans.
5 The players talked to the fans at the service station.
6 The players and fans travelled back to London on the same bus.

WRITING

8 Write a paragraph (120–150 words) about the first time you did something difficult, for example, rode a bike, went swimming in the sea, cooked a meal, or spoke English to a native speaker. Include this information.

- What it was
- How you felt before
- Any problems you had doing it
- How you felt when it was finished.

PRONUNCIATION

UNIT 1
Linking words with *up*

1 **Match the sentence halves.**

0	I find it difficult to get	*d*
1	I've got too much homework. I spend	
2	Hi, Kelly! What's	
3	Now that it's winter, why don't you take	
4	Last night we stayed	
5	We'd like you to come, but it's	
6	Have you seen Jim? I wonder what he's	
7	She's ninety now and isn't	
8	I don't want to move. If it was	
9	The test has started. Please pick	

a up? You look really sad!
b up your pen and start writing.
c up to me, I'd stay here.
d up early in the morning.
e up to going for long walks.
f up skiing? It's so much fun!
g up to three hours a night doing it.
h up late talking about our holidays.
i up to these days.
j up to you.

2 🔊05 **Listen, check and repeat.**

3 **Write the phrases with *up* in the column that corresponds to the correct linked sound.**

t pronounced	*get up*
d pronounced	
k pronounced	
s pronounced	
z pronounced	

4 🔊06 **Listen, check and repeat.**

UNIT 2
Initial consonant clusters with /s/

1 **Complete the words with the correct letters. These are all /s/ consonant clusters.**

0 I like the top that boy's wearing – the one with black and white ___*str*___ipes .
1 A _____ong wind was blowing from the east.
2 Her favourite shapes are circles and _____ares.
3 They heard a loud _____ash as the rock fell into the river.
4 She had a headache from looking at the computer _____een all morning.
5 The fire _____ead quickly because of the heat and wind.
6 The people were _____eaming on the roller coaster ride.

2 🔊08 **Listen, check and repeat.**

UNIT 3
Strong and weak forms: /ɒv/ and /əv/

1 **Match the questions and answers.**

0	What do you always buy the same brand **of**?	*c*
1	What are your favourite shoes made **of**?	
2	What kinds **of** clothes do you have the most **of**?	
3	Do you have a lot **of** gadgets?	
4	Which **of** your gadgets do you use the most?	

a My mobile phone. Most **of** my friends have one so we text each other a lot.
b They're made **of** leather and they've got rubber soles.
c Chocolate! I love the taste **of** Black & Green.
d I'm quite a casual person. I've got a lot **of** jeans and T-shirts.
e Not really. Most **of** them, like the computer and games console, belong to the whole family.

2 🔊12 **Listen and check.**

3 **Underline the weak forms and circle the strong forms of the word *of* in the sentences.**

4 🔊12 **Listen, check and repeat.**

UNIT 4
Consonant–vowel word linking

1 Underline the words where the final consonant is linked to the vowel sound in the next word.

0 I like that film. <u>It's about</u> two friends who go travelling.

1 I didn't find out who wrote the message.

2 My dad doesn't walk to work anymore.

3 Her family lived in Paris before they came to London.

4 They lost everything when their flat burned down.

5 Jenny's mum gets angry when she doesn't tidy her room.

6 Can we have our break now?

7 It was so difficult to make up my mind!

8 His friends felt awful when Tom told them they'd forgotten his birthday.

9 The climb was difficult, so she gave up before she got to the top.

2 🔊17 Listen, check and repeat.

3 Write the phrases with the linked sound in the correct column.

t pronounced	d pronounced	k pronounced	s pronounced	v pronounced
			it's about	

4 🔊18 Listen, check and repeat.

UNIT 5
The schwa /ə/ in word endings

1 Complete the words with the correct spelling.

-ure (x1) | -ent (x2) | -ion (x3) | -ate (x1)
-ous (x3) | -on (x1) | -an (x1) | -al (x3)
-el (x1) | -ul (x1) | -er (x1) | -or (x1)

0 The story will capture your attent *ion* and imaginat *ion* .

1 It's a historic_____ nov_____ about a desper_____ and danger_____ man.

2 Many fam_____ people live in centr_____ Lond_____.

3 The hospit_____ provided informat_____ about the accid_____.

4 They used a pict_____ of a beautif_____ old wom_____ for the advertisem_____.

5 She was the obvi_____ choice to direct anoth_____ horr_____ film.

2 Although the spelling is different, all of these words end with the same sound. What is it?

3 🔊21 Listen, check and repeat.

UNIT 6
The /ʒ/ phoneme

1 🔊22 Listen and circle the one word in each group which doesn't have the /ʒ/ phoneme.

0 A casual   B usually   C revision   Ⓓcaution

1 A sabotage   B version   C engine   D camouflage

2 A Asia   B Russia   C treasure   D collision

3 A magician   B illusionist   C occasion   D explosion

4 A pleasure   B television   C pleasant   D decision

5 A confusion   B revision   C measure   D permission

6 A unusual   B mansion   C vision   D leisure

7 A exposure   B usual   C fashion   D diversion

8 A erosion   B decoration   C illusion   D invasion

2 🔊22 Listen again, check and repeat.

3 Complete the sentences with the words in the list.

~~revision~~ | Asia | casual | pleasure | decision
illusionist | occasion | collision | version | usually

0 I need to do a lot of __*revision*__ because we have a test tomorrow.

1 I don't _____ have to study more than an hour at the weekend.

2 A   Thank you for helping me today.
B   It's a _____.

3 There was a terrible _____ on the motorway today, but no one was hurt.

4 Dynamo is an amazing _____.

5 I'm saving this beautiful dress to wear for a special _____.

6 I liked that film, but I prefer the original _____.

7 I've always wanted to travel around _____.

8 It wasn't an easy _____, but I finally chose a career in biology.

9 She prefers _____ clothes and wears jeans and T-shirts most of the time.

4 🔊23 Listen, check and repeat.

UNIT 7
Intonation – inviting, accepting and refusing invitations

1 🔊 28 **Listen to the dialogues. For each one, decide if the speaker is accepting or refusing the invitation and tick the correct box.**

0 Would you like to come with us to see a film on Saturday?

Accepting ✓   Refusing ☐

1 Would you like to work on the history project with me?

Accepting ☐   Refusing ☐

2 Those bags look heavy. Can I help you carry them?

Accepting ☐   Refusing ☐

3 I'm going to ride my bike to the river and go for a swim. Do you want to come?

Accepting ☐   Refusing ☐

4 Didn't you bring anything to eat? Would you like half of my cheese sandwich?

Accepting ☐   Refusing ☐

5 I'm having some friends around for dinner next Saturday. Why don't you join us?

Accepting ☐   Refusing ☐

2 🔊 29 **Look at these extracts from the dialogues. For each one, is the speaker accepting (A) or refusing (R) the invitation? Listen to the extracts to check your answers.**

1 I'd love to come! ☐

2 I'm sorry, Pete. ☐

3 That's very kind of you. ☐

4 That's a great idea. ☐

5 Oh thank you ☐

6 What a pity! ☐

3 **Underline the stressed words in each of the sentences in Exercise 2 and circle the correct word to complete the rule.**

Intonation goes *up / down* when accepting an invitation.
Intonation goes *up / down* when refusing an invitation.

4 🔊 29 **Listen, check and repeat.**

UNIT 8
Intonation – expressing surprise

1 🔊 32 **Read and listen to the dialogue, ignoring the spaces and answer this question. Why didn't Harriet hold the ladder?**

~~believe~~ | ambulance | arm | bookshop
crash | English | highest | ladder (x2)
later | mobile | Tell | that | way

ANNA You're not going to ⁰ *believe* this, but…

BEN ¹_____ me.

ANNA Well, Harriet was at the ²_____ yesterday and she asked the shop assistant for the new ³_____ Course Book. It was on the ⁴_____ shelf in the shop!

BEN Right.

ANNA So, the assistant had to get it down using a ⁵_____. The next thing Harriet knew, he'd fallen and broken his ⁶_____!

BEN No! How did ⁷_____ happen?

ANNA He asked Harriet to hold the ⁸_____ but she thought he told her to come back ⁹_____. As she was leaving, she heard this terrible ¹⁰_____!

BEN Really?

ANNA Yes! at least she had her ¹¹_____. She had to ring for an ¹²_____!

BEN No ¹³_____!

2 🔊 32 **Complete the spaces. Listen again and check.**

3 🔊 33 **Ben changes his intonation to express surprise. Listen again, try to notice this, and repeat.**

UNIT 9
Moving word stress

1 🔊 35 **Listen and mark the stress.**

0	congrátulate (v)	congratulátions (n)
1	navigate (v)	navigation (n)
2	mystery (n)	mysterious (adj)
3	artist (n)	artistic (adj)
4	present (v)	present (n)
5	photograph (n)	photography (n)
6	explain (v)	explanation (n)
7	investigate (v)	investigation (n)
8	electric (adj)	electricity (n)
9	music (n)	musician (n)

2 🔊 35 **Listen again, check and repeat.**

3 Write the names of the people who do these jobs. Use a dictionary to help you.

0 art   *artist*
1 music   _____
2 navigation   _____
3 present (v)   _____
4 investigate   _____
5 electric   _____
6 research (v)   _____

4 🔊36 Listen, check and repeat. Circle the stressed syllable in each of the jobs.

UNIT 10
Short and long vowel sounds: /ɪ/ – /iː/ and /ɒ/ – /əʊ/

1 🔊40 Listen and circle the word you hear.

0 ship – (sheep)   5 not – note
1 sit – seat   6 hop – hope
2 slip – sleep   7 clock – cloak
3 chip – cheap   8 want – won't
4 will – we'll   9 sock – soak

2 Choose one word from each pair in Exercise 1 to complete the sentences.

0 My room's such a mess that I can't find my other _sock_ !
1 Oh my goodness. Look at the _____ – it's time to go home.
2 Now that it's stopped raining, _____ have to go.
3 We're going to the beach and I _____ you can come with us.
4 Her grandparents are _____ farmers.
5 Please _____ down. The doctor will see you in a moment.
6 Danny _____ go to the cinema with us if we decide to see a horror film.
7 I love my new jumper. And it was _____, too.
8 It's important to get about 8 hours _____ a night.
9 Please make a _____ in your diaries that we don't have a class on Monday.

3 🔊41 Listen, check and repeat.

UNIT 11
Strong and weak forms: /tuː/ and /tə/

1 Match the questions and answers.

0 Do you think it's easy **to** make friends when you move **to** a new place?   `d`
1 If it was up **to** you, would you go **to** a hot or cold place for your holiday?   ☐
2 Would you star in a film, if you were asked **to**?   ☐
3 Before coming **to** class, who was the last person you spoke **to**?   ☐
4 Which person, living or dead, do you most look up **to**?   ☐
5 What kind of a book would you write, if you had **to**?   ☐

a I'd go **to** the mountains – it would be great **to** go skiing this winter!
b I talked **to** my mum on my mobile – she wanted **to** know if I was coming home for lunch.
c Perhaps my grandmother – she's so kind and fun **to** be with.
d It depends on the place you move **to**. I think it's easier if you go **to** a large town or city.
e I don't think so – I don't even like going **to** the cinema.
f Historical fiction, I think. I often think about what it would be like **to** live in the past.

2 🔊43 Listen and check your answers.

3 Underline the weak forms and circle the strong forms of *to* in the sentences in Exercise 1.

4 🔊43 Listen again and check your answers.

UNIT 12
Different pronunciations of *ea*

1 Write the words in the correct columns.

bread | break | breakfast | breathe | clean
early | easy | healthy | heard | please
research | speak | steak | sweating | wear

1 /iː/ **eat**	2 /e/ **head**	3 /ɜː/ **learn**	4 /eɪ/ **great**	5 /eə/ **bear**
	bread			

2 🔊45 Listen, check and repeat.

GRAMMAR REFERENCE

UNIT 1
Present tenses (review)

To talk about the present, we mostly use the following tenses: present simple, present continuous, present perfect simple and present perfect continuous

1. We use the present simple to talk about facts and give opinions, and to talk about regular habits.

   It **takes** around four minutes to boil an egg. (fact)
   I **think** this is awful. (opinion)
   I usually **go** to bed around 11 o'clock. (habit)

2. We use the present continuous to talk about what's happening at or around the time of speaking.

   What **are** you **doing**?
   A TV company **is making** a programme about life plans.

3. We use the present perfect simple to talk about past actions and experiences but without saying exactly when. This tense links the present and the past and we often use it when a past event has an effect on the present.

   She**'s read** lots of articles about this and she**'s learned** a lot.
   The storm **has caused** a lot of flooding in the town.

4. We use the present perfect continuous to talk about actions that started in the past and are still happening.

   I**'ve been trying** to get fitter for several weeks now.

Future tenses (review)

To talk about the future, we mostly use the following tenses: present continuous, will / won't (do) and going to (do)

1. We often use the present continuous to talk about future plans and arrangements.

   I**'m having** a guitar lesson tomorrow morning.

2. We often use will / won't (do) to make predictions.

   She's very clever – I'm sure she**'ll do** really well at university
   This is the dry time of year – it **won't rain** again until September.

3. We often use going to (do) to talk about intentions.

   Next year, I**'m going to start** university.
   Where **are** you **going to** go on holiday next year?

UNIT 2
Narrative tenses (review)

To talk about the past and to tell narratives, we mostly use the following tenses: past simple, past continuous, past perfect simple and past perfect continuous

1. We use the past simple to talk about actions that happened at one moment in the past, or were true at one time in the past.

   I **fell** over.
   People **didn't have** easy lives two hundred years ago.

2. We use the past continuous to describe ongoing actions or situations around a time in the past.

   I **was running** really fast (and I fell over).
   Thousands of people **were living** in very enclosed spaces.

   We also use the past continuous to talk about an ongoing action that was interrupted by another.

   The fire started while people **were sleeping**.

3. We use the past perfect to describe an event that happened before another.

   The weather **had been** very hot when the fire broke out.
   When we arrived, the film **had** already **started**.

4. We use the past perfect continuous to talk about ongoing actions that began before another action in the past.

   When I finished the race I was exhausted because I**'d been running** for more than two hours.
   He couldn't answer the teacher's question because he **hadn't been listening**.

would and used to

1. We use the expression used to + verb to talk about habits and customs in the past that are no longer true.

   My dad **used to play football**. (= My dad played football in the past but he doesn't any more.)
   When I was a kid, I **used to listen** to pop music. (= That was my habit but I don't do this any more.)

2 It is also possible to use *would* + verb to talk about habits and customs in the past.

*My mum **would cook** chicken every Sunday. (= This was a custom of my mum's.)*
*At school, I **would** always **ask** the teacher questions. (= This was a habit of mine when I was a schoolchild.)*

3 The difference between *used to* and *would* is that we can only use *would* for repeated actions – we cannot use it for a permanent state or situation.

*He **used to be** a police officer. (A permanent state)*
*When I was little, I **used to play** in the garden a lot. (A repeated action)*

UNIT 3
(don't) have to / ought to / should(n't) / must

1 We use *have to* to say 'this is important or necessary'. We use *must* to say that we, or other people, have an obligation to do something.

*Our train leaves at 7 o'clock, so I **have to get up** early.*
*I **must save** some money for mum's birthday present.*
*You **must try** to work harder, Jack.*

2 We use *don't have to* to say this is NOT important or necessary.

*You **don't have to come** with us if you don't want to.*

3 We use *should* or *ought to* to tell someone that something is a good idea.

*At the beach you **should put** some sun cream on.*
*That wasn't a nice thing to say – you **ought to say** sorry.*

Remember: *ought to* isn't as frequent as *should*. It is used mostly in writing, and the negative form is rare.

4 We use *shouldn't* to tell someone that something is not a good idea.

*You **shouldn't spend** so much on clothes.*

had ('d) better (not)

We use *had / 'd better (not)* to advise or warn people in strong terms. It is used to tell people about negative results in the future if they do / don't do something.

The form is always past (*had*) and it is often shortened to *'d*.

*You**'d better** hurry up (or you'll miss the train).*
*He**'d better not** say that again (or I will be very angry).*

can('t) / must(n't)

1 When we want to talk or ask about permission, we often use the modal verb *can / can't*.

*You **can go** to the party but you **can't stay** late.*
***Can** I **borrow** your phone to make a call?*

2 To say what isn't allowed, we use *can't* or *mustn't*.

*You **can't park** here. (This is a fact / rule.)*
*You **mustn't leave** your things on the floor! (The speaker isn't allowing something.)*

UNIT 4
First and second conditional (review)

1 We use the first conditional to talk about real situations and their consequences. It consists of two clauses. The *if* + present simple clause introduces the possible situation or condition. The *will / won't* clause gives the result or consequence.

*If you **leave** that door open, the cat **will get** out.*
*If we **don't leave** now, we **won't get** to school on time.*

2 We use the second conditional to talk about hypothetical or very unlikely situations and their (imaginary) consequences. It consists of two clauses. The *if* + past simple clause introduces the hypothetical situation. The *would* clause gives the imagined result or consequence.

*If I **had** a cat, I**'d call** it Max. (I don't have a cat.)*
*If we **didn't have** a cat, we **wouldn't have to** spend money on cat food. (We have a cat and we need to spend money on cat food.)*

Time conjunctions

We can join ideas about future actions or situations using words like: *if, unless, until, when, as soon as*

When we use these words, we use them with the present simple tense (not *will / won't*) even though the clause refers to the future.

*She won't be happy **if** you **forget** her birthday.*
*We'll be late **unless** we **leave** now.*
*I won't stop asking you **until** you **tell** me.*
*They'll be hungry **when** they **get** here.*
*I'll call you **as soon as** I **finish** this work.*

wish and if only

1 We use *wish* or *if only* + past simple to say that we would like a present situation to be different from what it actually is.

*I **wish** I **had** more friends. (I don't have many friends.)*
*My friends **wish** they **were** rich. (They aren't rich.)*

2 We use *wish / if only* + *could* to talk about wanting to have the ability or permission to do something.

*I **wish** I **could** speak Italian.*
***If only** you **could** come with me.*

3 If there is a situation we don't like (for example, someone is doing or always does something that annoys us) we can use *wish / if only* + *would(n't)*.

*I **wish** you **would knock** before coming into my room.*
***If only** he **wouldn't talk** about football all the time!*

Third conditional (review)

We use the third conditional to talk about how things might have been different in the past. The third conditional is formed with *If* + past perfect + *would (not) have* + past participle. The third conditional talks about impossible conditions (because the past cannot be changed).

If I'd been careful, I wouldn't have dropped the camera.
(I wasn't careful, so I dropped the camera.)
If you hadn't woken me up, I would have slept for hours.
(You woke me up so I didn't sleep for hours.)

UNIT 5
Relative pronouns

We use relative pronouns to start a relative clause.

1 To refer to people, we use *who* or *that*.

He's a writer. He wrote that fantastic story.
→ *He's the writer who / that wrote that fantastic story.*

2 To refer to things, we use *which* or *that*.

It's a great story. It was made into a film.
→ *It's a great story that / which was made into a film.*

3 To refer to possessions, we use *whose*.

I know a boy. His sister is on TV.
→ *I know a boy whose sister is on TV.*

4 To refer to places, we use *where*.

This is the town. I was born here.
→ *This is the town where I was born.*

Defining and non-defining relative clauses

There are two kinds of relative clause: <u>defining</u> and <u>non-defining</u>.

1 A defining relative clause identifies an object, a person, a place or a possession. We need this information to know who or what is being talked about. When we write these sentences, we don't use any commas.

The woman was a genius. She wrote this book.
→ *The woman who wrote this book was a genius.*
I saw a film last night. The film was terrible.
→ *The film that I saw last night was terrible.*

2 We use non-defining relative clauses to add extra information, which is not needed to understand the sentence. We put commas around these clauses when we write them. They are rarely used in conversational language.

My uncle lives in Sydney. He's a very successful writer. → *My uncle, who lives in Sydney, is a very successful writer.*

Relative clauses with *which*

1 When we want to refer back to a whole idea or clause, we use the relative pronoun *which*.

He went into the desert alone. It was a dangerous thing to do.
→ *He went into the desert alone, which was a dangerous thing to do.*

2 We cannot use *that* or *what* in this way – only *which*.

Stephen King has sold millions of books, which (~~that~~ / ~~what~~) has made him very rich.

UNIT 6
Present and past passive (review)

1 We use the passive (present or past) to say what happens or happened to the subject of the sentence. Often the cause of the action is unknown or unimportant.

2 We form the passive with a form of the verb *be* and the past participle of the verb.

English and French are spoken in Canada.
The roof of the house was destroyed in the storm.

3 We use the preposition *by* to say who or what does the action, but only if this is important.

My bike was stolen. (We don't know, or it isn't important, who stole it.)
The magic show was watched by over five hundred people. (It's important to say who watched the show.)

have something done

1 We use the structure *have something done* when we talk about someone else doing a function or service for us.

My granny's very old so she has her meals cooked for her. (Another person cooks her meals for her.)
They had their car repaired. (They paid a mechanic to repair their car.)

2 It is formed with *have* + noun + past participle.

I had my phone repaired last week.

3 In less formal contexts, *get* often replaces *have*.

I'm going to get my hair done for the party tonight.

Future and Present perfect passive (review)

1 The future passive is formed with *will be / won't be* + past participle.

The new supermarket will be opened next week by a famous TV actor.

2 The present perfect passive is formed with *have / has (not) been* + past participle.

The streets of our town look awful – they haven't been cleaned for two weeks.

UNIT 7

make / let and be allowed to

1 We use *make (someone do)* to talk about forcing someone to do something that perhaps they don't want to do.

*Our school **makes us wear** a uniform. (= We cannot choose, it's an obligation that our school gives us.)*
*My sister **made me clean** her bike. (= I could not choose, my sister forced me.)*

2 We use *let (someone do)* to talk about permission to do the things we want to do.

*Our parents **let us sleep** late on Sundays. (= Our parents give us permission to sleep late.)*
*I **let my brother use** my laptop at the weekend. (= I gave my brother permission to use my laptop.)*

3 We use *(not) be allowed to (do something)* to say that someone has (or has not) got permission.

*Are we **allowed to use** our mobile phones in here?*
*When my parents were children, they **weren't allowed to go** out at night.*

be / get used to

1 To say that we are (not) accustomed to or (not) comfortable with doing certain things, we can use the expressions *be used to* and *get used to*.

2 *be used to* refers to a state.

*She's **not used to eating** dinner so late.*

3 *get used to* refers to the change from something we weren't used to, to a situation that we are used to now.

*It took her a long time to **get used to wearing** glasses.*

4 These expressions are followed by a noun or noun phrase, or the gerund (*-ing*) form of a verb.

*The animals are not used to **people touching them**.*
*I'm getting used to **speaking** in public now.*

UNIT 8

Reported speech (review)

We use reported speech to report what someone said in the past. In reported speech, we often change the verb that was used in direct speech.

*'It's 10 o'clock,' she said. → She said it **was** 10 o'clock.*
*'It's raining,' my mum said. → My mum said it **was raining**.*
*'I've had a really bad day,' he said. → He said he'**d had** a really bad day.*
*'He didn't remember to phone me,' I said. → I said he **hadn't remembered** to phone me.*
*'I can't do this exercise,' my friend said. → My friend said she **couldn't do** the exercise.*
*'I'll pick you up at eight,' she said. → She said she **would pick** me up at eight.*
*'We're going to tell the police,' she said. → She said they **were going** to tell the police.*

But sometimes the tense doesn't change.

*'They'd stolen my car,' she said. → She said they'**d stolen** her car.*
*'No one would want it to happen,' he said. → He said that no one **would** want it to happen.*

Reported questions, requests and imperatives

1 With reported questions, we use statement word order and NOT question word order. We also do not use a question mark.

*She asked me **who my friends were**.*
(NOT They asked me ~~who were my friends~~.)
*I asked her **what she did**.*
(NOT I asked her ~~what did she do~~.)
*They asked me **why I wanted the job**.*
(NOT They asked me ~~why did I want the job~~.)

2 When we report yes / no questions, we use *if* (or *whether*) and statement word order.

'Is that book good?'
*→ She asked me **if the book was** good.*
'Do you eat fish?'
*→ He asked me **whether I ate fish**.*

3 When we report *wh-* questions (with *who / where / what / how / when* etc.), we use the same question word and statement word order.

'What are you looking at?'
*→ He asked me **what I was looking at**.*
'Why did you leave the door open?'
*→ They asked me **why I had left the door open**.*
'How much money did they steal?'
*→ They asked me **how much money they'd stolen**.*

4 With requests, we use *asked* + person + *to (do)*.

'Please help me with this, Mum.'
*→ He **asked his mum to help** him.*
'Can you close the door, please?'
*→ She **asked me to close** the door.*

5 With imperatives, we use *told* + person + *(not) to (do)*

'Go away!'
→ He told me to go away.
'Don't phone the police!'
→ They told me not to phone the police.

UNIT 9
Modals of deduction (present)

Sometimes we express an opinion about whether something is true or not now, based on what we know or can see. We use the modal verbs *must / can't / might / could*.

1   When we're sure that something is true, we often use *must* + verb.

    *They live in a really big house – they **must have** a lot of money.*

2   When we're sure that something isn't true, we often use *can't* + verb.

    *That cheese is two weeks old, so it **can't be** good any more.*

3   When we aren't sure, we often use *might* or *could* + verb, to show our uncertainty.

    *They're speaking Portuguese, so they **might be** Brazilian.*
    *Perhaps we shouldn't go in there – it **could be** dangerous.*

Modal verbs of deduction (past)

Sometimes we express an opinion about a past situation or event, based on what we know or can see now. We use the modal verbs *must / can't / might / could* + *have* + past participle.

*The wind blew this tree down. It **must have been** really strong.*
*The door lock isn't broken, so the thieves **can't have got in** that way.*
*I'm not sure when my bike was stolen but it **might have been** yesterday afternoon.*
*Police think that the criminals **could have taken** more than a million dollars.*

should(n't) have

We use *should / shouldn't have (done)* to criticise things that we, or other people, did in the past.

*You **should have come** to the party. (= You <u>didn't</u> come to the party, and I think that was a mistake.)*
*They **should have won**. (= They <u>didn't</u> win, and I think that was bad / wrong.)*
*You **shouldn't have taken** it without asking me. (= You <u>did</u> take it without asking me, and that was wrong.)*
*I **shouldn't have said** that. (= I <u>did</u> say it, and I think that I was wrong to do so.)*

UNIT 10
Future continuous

We use the future continuous to talk about things that will be in progress at a specified time in the future. The future continuous is formed by *will* + *be* + the *-ing* form of the verb.

*This time next week, I**'ll be sitting** on a beach in Italy.*
*Twenty years from now, we **won't be using** money to buy things any more.*

Future perfect

If we want to talk about an action that will have been completed at a specified time in the future, we use the future perfect tense. The future perfect tense is formed by *will* + the present perfect.

*Some people think that by 2050, credit cards **will have disappeared**.*
*By Saturday, I**'ll have spent** all my money – so I won't be able to go out on Sunday.*

UNIT 11
Verbs followed by gerund or infinitive

Some verbs in English are followed by *to* + infinitive, some are followed by a gerund (the *-ing* form of a verb).

1   Some common verbs followed by *to* + infinitive are: *afford, choose, decide, expect, hope, learn, offer, promise, want*.

    *The show's too expensive – I can't **afford to go**.*
    *The other player's really good, so I don't **expect to win** the match.*
    *You need to **learn to control** yourself and not get so angry.*
    *I **promise to be** there on time.*

2   Some common verbs followed by a gerund are: *avoid, enjoy, feel like, finish, imagine, (don't) mind, miss, practise, suggest*.

    *That park's a bit dangerous, so we **avoid going** there.*
    *I don't want to work any more – I **feel like doing** something to enjoy myself.*
    *I can't **imagine living** in a foreign country.*
    *Do you ever **miss seeing** your friends when you travel?*

to / in order to / so as to

1 When we want to give the reason why someone did something (the purpose), we can use *to* + infinitive. We can also use *in order to* or *so as to* – these are more formal.

   *I phoned her **to ask** about her about her holiday.*
   *It is important to arrive early **in order to save** time.*
   *Please fill in this form **so as to help** us to provide the best service for you.*

2 When we want to make *in order to* or *so as to* negative, we put *not* before *to*.

   *Please speak quietly **in order not to disturb** other users of the library.*
   *Please switch off your mobile phones **so as not to spoil** the film for other people.*

so and such

1 We can use *so* or *such* to emphasise adjectives, adverbs, nouns and noun phrases.

   *That's **so expensive**!*
   *You walk **so quickly**!*
   *He's **such a fool**.*
   *It's **such an interesting place** to visit.*

2 We also use *so* / *such* to show how one thing is the result of another. We use *so* with adjectives and adverbs, and *such (a)* with nouns.

   *It was **so expensive** that I couldn't afford to buy it.*
   *You walk **so quickly** that I can't keep up with you.*
   *He's **such a fool** that I never talk to him.*

3 We connect the ideas with the word *that*, but it can be left out.

   *The book was so boring (**that**) I didn't finish it.*

UNIT 12
Phrasal verbs

A phrasal verb is a combination of a verb with a preposition or an adverb – this creates a new verb which often has a meaning that is completely different from the verb alone. For example, the verb 'look' means 'use your eyes in order to see something', but the phrasal verb 'look after' means 'to take care of someone or something'. Phrasal verbs are very frequent in both spoken and written English.

1 Most phrasal verbs have two parts.

   *I can't **work out** the answer. (find by thinking)*
   *I always **look after** other people's things. (take care of)*

2 With some phrasal verbs, the two parts can be separated by the object of the verb.

   *I **worked out** the answer. OR I **worked** the answer **out**.*

   However, when the object is a pronoun, it must come between the two parts.

   *I **worked it out**. (NOT I worked out it.)*

3 In other phrasal verbs, these parts can never be separated.

   *I **look after** my clothes. (NOT I look my clothes after.)*

4 To find out if a phrasal verb can be split or not, look in a dictionary:

   If it <u>can</u> be split, it will be listed: work <u>st</u> out
   If it <u>can't</u> be split, it will be listed: look after <u>sb</u>

5 Some phrasal verbs have more than one meaning.

   *My car's **broken down**. (stopped working)*
   *When she heard the news, she **broke down**. (started crying).*

I wish / If only + past perfect

We use *I wish* or *If only* + past perfect to express regret about past actions or events.

*I wish I'**d been nice** to her. (= I <u>wasn't</u> nice to her, and I am sorry about it.)*
*I wish you **hadn't opened** it. (= You opened it, and I am sorry about it.)*
*If only I'**d listened** to my parents. (= I <u>didn't</u> listen to them, and I regret it.)*
*If only we **hadn't missed** the bus. (= We missed the bus, and I regret it.)*

IRREGULAR VERBS

Base form	Past simple	Past participle
be	was / were	been
beat	beat	beaten
become	became	become
begin	began	begun
bite	bit	bitten
blow	blew	blown
break	broke	broken
breed	bred	bred
bring	brought	brought
build	built	built
burn	burned / burnt	burned / burnt
buy	bought	bought
can	could	–
catch	caught	caught
choose	chose	chosen
come	came	come
cost	cost	cost
cut	cut	cut
do	did	done
draw	drew	drawn
dream	dreamed / dreamt	dreamed / dreamt
drink	drank	drunk
drive	drove	driven
eat	ate	eaten
fall	fell	fallen
feel	felt	felt
fight	fought	fought
find	found	found
flee	fled	fled
fly	flew	flown
forget	forgot	forgotten
forgive	forgave	forgiven
freeze	froze	frozen
get	got	got
give	gave	given
go	went	gone
grow	grew	grown
hang	hung	hung
have	had	had
hear	heard	heard
hide	hid	hidden
hit	hit	hit
hold	held	held
hurt	hurt	hurt
keep	kept	kept
know	knew	known
lay	laid	laid
lead	led	led
learn	learned / learnt	learned / learnt
leave	left	left

Base form	Past simple	Past participle
lend	lent	lent
let	let	let
lie	lay	lain
light	lit	lit
lose	lost	lost
make	made	made
mean	meant	meant
meet	met	met
pay	paid	paid
put	put	put
quit	quit	quit
read	read	read
ride	rode	ridden
ring	rang	rung
rise	rose	risen
run	ran	run
say	said	said
see	saw	seen
seek	sought	sought
sell	sold	sold
send	sent	sent
set	set	set
shake	shook	shaken
shoot	shot	shot
show	showed	shown
shut	shut	shut
sing	sang	sung
sink	sank	sunk
sit	sat	sat
sleep	slept	slept
speak	spoke	spoken
spend	spent	spent
spill	spilled / spilt	spilled / spilt
spread	spread	spread
stand	stood	stood
steal	stole	stolen
stick	stuck	stuck
strike	struck	struck
swim	swam	swum
swing	swung	swung
take	took	taken
teach	taught	taught
tell	told	told
think	thought	thought
throw	threw	thrown
understand	understood	understood
wake	woke	woken
wear	wore	worn
win	won	won
write	wrote	written